Renewing the Face of the Earth

David Atkinson is the Bishop of Thetford and a pastoral theologian and ethicist. A research chemist prior to his ordination, he taught Christian ethics and psychology of religion at Corpus Christi College, Oxford.

He is the author of numerous books, and was one of the editors of *The New Dictionary of Christian Ethics and Pastoral Theology* (IVP).

Renewing the Face of the Earth

A Theological and Pastoral Response to Climate Change

David Atkinson

© David Atkinson 2008

First published in 2008 by the Canterbury Press Norwich
(a publishing imprint of Hymns Ancient & Modern Limited,
a registered charity)
13–17 Long Lane, London EC1A 9PN

www.scm-canterburypress.co.uk

All rights reserved. No part of this publication may be
reproduced, stored in a retrieval system, or transmitted,
in any form or by any means, electronic, mechanical,
photocopying or otherwise, without the prior permission of
the publisher, Canterbury Press.

The Author has asserted his right under the Copyright,
Designs and Patents Act, 1988, to be identified as the
Author of this Work

Scripture quotations are from the New Revised Standard
Version of the Bible, copyright 1989 by the Division of Christian
Education of the National Council of the Churches of Christ in
the USA. Used by permission. All rights reserved.

Prayers from *Common Worship: Services and Prayers for the
Church of England* (2000) are copyright © The Archbishops'
Council and are reproduced by permission.

British Library Cataloguing in Publication data

A catalogue record for this book is available
from the British Library

ISBN 978-1-85311-898-2

Typeset by Regent Typesetting, London
Printed in the UK by CPI William Clowes
Beccles NR34 7TL

To my grandchildren,
Tom, Charlotte, Bethia, Jessie and Alfie-Louise,
with love and prayers and hope.

Contents

Acknowledgements ix

1 Global warming is changing more than the climate 1
2 Cosmic Covenant 29
3 Creation: the context for covenant 47
4 Sabbath: covenant joy 71
5 Justice: allegiance to the covenant Lord 93
6 Redemption: covenant hope 121
7 Gift and calling: living as God's covenant people 140

Further Reading and Resources 162

Acknowledgements

I am very grateful to Bishop Graham James, Bishop of Norwich, for allowing me two months' study leave in which to complete this book. I am indebted to the members of the Diocese of Norwich Environment Group for their stimulus and encouragement. I would also particularly like to express my thanks to Professor Mike Hulme, of the School of Environmental Sciences at the University of East Anglia, who was the founding Director (2000–2007) of the Tyndall Centre for Climate Change Research, to Dr Keith Tovey, Reader in Environmental Sciences at the UEA, and also to my wife, Dr Sue Atkinson, for their encouragement, critique and suggestions on various parts of the text.

I

Global warming is changing more than the climate

It is time the Christian Church woke up to the urgency of climate change.

Of course, this is true for everyone, but I want to argue that the Christian Church holds a distinct theological vision of the world and of humanity which makes the questions posed by climate change particularly urgent ones for us. The Church has a God-given responsibility to bear witness to the truth of the Gospel in relation to the world God has created and to our place within it. And the Church has a particular opportunity to bear that witness, which I believe to be increasingly urgent.

Many Christian people are already wide awake, and working hard, as I shall illustrate further in a moment. But there are many Christian people who are not persuaded about the seriousness of climate change and who either think that we should not be wasting our time on such questions, or believe that it does not really concern them. For example, a priest writing in *The Church of England Newspaper* in November 2007 argued that the time and effort being spent on responding to global warming is mistaken. He wrote that even if the world is warming (which he did not seem too sure about), there is nothing for us to do: 'We cannot "fight global warming" any more than Canute could turn back the tide. God is the God of the climate as well as of the Universe. So don't let's waste time and resources on such matters.' Someone else replied in the same vein that 'We should not allow ourselves to become obsessed with "saving the planet" instead of bringing in the Kingdom of God, with special emphasis on the Gospel of Jesus Christ.'

These letters assume a certain theology of God's relationship with the world and with humanity, which seems to say 'God is sovereign; all things are in God's hands; it is sheer presumption on our part to think that we can make any difference to the way the world is, and it is not our job anyway, so let's leave things to God and get on with preaching the Gospel'.

I think these letter writers are wrong. I want in this book to argue that a more fully biblical theology of covenant and creation commits us to respond urgently to the questions posed by climate change, and that such a response is centrally part of the meaning of the Gospel of a God who 'so loved the world'.

I am writing this book also for a woman student in a class I taught in the USA when I was exploring some of these ideas. She came from a conservative Christian group which identified with the Republican Party, and told me that in her church anything to do with 'the environment' was so associated with the Democrats – and therefore, she said, with 'liberal theology' – that no one took it seriously. I want to argue that the issues are far more serious than party politics. Love for our neighbours must not be constrained by the narrow limits of our party-political thinking.

I also have in mind the bloggers on a conservative Christian website who came across an article I had written on these themes and commented that people like 'the good bishop' should not 'stray into areas that aren't ones in which they are expert. The problem is not as simple as the good bishop would want his readers to assume.' And again, 'reading the good bishop's comments is a painful example of C.S. Lewis' comment that clergy are trained to care for those of us who are going to live forever, and that we do them an injustice in expecting them to provide leadership in secular matters beyond their competence'. In other words, let Church leaders keep out of commenting on 'secular' matters and instead get on with pastoral care. Many of the bloggers suggested that the science is inconclusive, that the 'global warming lobby' is politically motivated, and that really there is not much to worry about. Well, I am not a climate scientist (my own research was in organic chemistry and X-ray crystallography), but I can read Sir John Houghton's authoritative book, *Global Warming: The Complete Briefing*,[1] and find it very persuasive. But one of my main issues with the bloggers is the assumption that Christian pastoral care somehow has nothing at all to do with living in the world God has made. I want to argue that such a divide between the 'sacred' and the 'secular' is actually a denial of the richness of the Gospel.

I had a similar experience at a major conference on climate change which I attended as a bishop of the Church of England along with scientists, economists, educators, journalists and many others. I happened to speak to the environment correspondent of a national daily newspaper who greeted me warmly, but then expressed considerable surprise at what a bishop was doing there. He could not understand what possible interest the Church might have in such a conference. So this book is also written for him.

I have written this with another group in mind – those Christians who believe that global warming is one of the 'signs of the times' that Jesus predicted about the end of the world. I saw a poster from a Christian group which read 'Global Warming? Rejoice! Droughts, floods, ecological disasters are signs of Jesus' return. Praise God!' There are, of course, just a few texts in the New Testament which could feed into this sort of off-beam theology, and we will need to look at them in due course. There is a widespread – and I think mistaken – assumption, for example, that the text in 2 Peter about 'all these things' being 'dissolved' (3.11) means that the life of the planet is all but over, and therefore there is little point in taking human care of the environment seriously at all. I want in this book to present a richer theology of resurrection which means that what we do to God's earth matters very much.

---

1 John Houghton, *Global Warming*, 2004.

I am also writing for the huge numbers of 'ordinary' Christian people who are faithfully getting on with loving God and serving their neighbours, and who are either confused about this whole debate, or so tired of being pressurized to 'go green' that any sense of urgency has been drained away. They know there is something important going on, but are at a loss to understand how their tiny contribution can make any difference at all, so they just get on with life and wish it would all go away. I believe we 'ordinary' Christian people need to wake up to the urgency of climate change.

Many Christians are awake

There is a very great deal of Christian work already going on. For example, Christian Aid[2] has, together with other relief agencies, been at the forefront of a Christian concern for the alleviation of poverty for many years, and has more recently been arguing for a close link between development issues and environmental issues, and that climate change raises moral questions of justice. The World Council of Churches has also linked environmental concerns with issues of sustainable development in many of its publications. A variety of Christian groups have been promoting environmental concerns and encouraging Christian people to respond creatively to climate change. For example, A Rocha[3] was launched in 2001 as an educational organization primarily working to promote 'creation care' through respect and enjoyment of local environments. The Christian Ecology Link[4] is older, an ecumenical group committed to helping Christian people integrate awareness of their

---

2 For example, the Christian Aid reports: *The Climate of Poverty*, 2006; Paula Clifford, *'All creation groaning'*, 2007; *The Human Face of Climate Change*, 2007.

3 A Rocha, 13 Avenue Road, Southall, Middlesex. UB1 3BL; www.arocha.org

4 Christian Ecology Link, 3 Bond Street, Lancaster LA1 3ER; www.christian-ecology.org.uk

impact on the environment into their faith and their lifestyle. Operation Noah[5] was founded as a joint project of the Christian Ecology Link and the Environmental Issues Network of Churches Together in Britain and Ireland (CTBI). It seeks to encourage 'churches and governments to lead a radical transformation in both our culture and economic systems; a transformation towards simpler, liveable and supportable lifestyles that will increase happiness and well-being, while safeguarding the whole of God's creation for future generations'.

The Conservation Foundation[6] has worked in partnership with churches as an educational and awareness-raising programme, helping to make links between industry and commerce, the world of education and the environment. Eco-Congregation[7] is a resource for churches, using an environmental audit and providing resources for education and for worship.

Among the many scientists who are Christians writing on these matters, let me single out just two. One is Professor R.J. Berry, who was Professor of Genetics at University College, London, from 1978 to 2000, President of the Linnean Society, the British Ecological Society, the European Ecological Federation, and Christians in Science. He has written widely on environmental issues and 'green theology'. His prestigious Gifford Lectures from 2003, published as *God's Book of Works: The Nature and Theology of Nature*,[8] bring environmental science and Christian faith together. 'Sam' Berry was also instrumental in drawing together in 1994 an international 'Evangelical Declaration on the Care of Creation'[9] setting out Christian affirmations relevant to discernible violations of creation, and identifying spiritual responses which it urges

---

5 Operation Noah; www.operationnoah.org
6 The Conservation Foundation, 1 Kensington Gore, London SW7 2AR; www.conservationfoundation.co.uk
7 Eco-Congregation, The Arthur Rank Centre, Stoneleigh Park, Warwickshire CV8 2LZ; www.ecocongregation.org
8 R.J. Berry, *God's Book of Works*, 2003.
9 Published in R.J. Berry (ed.), *The Care of Creation*, 2000, which is a collection of evangelical essays on the theme of the Declaration.

Christian people to adopt. The other scientist is Sir John Houghton, another evangelical Christian, who was Professor of Atmospheric Physics at Oxford before becoming Director General of the UK Meteorological Office from 1983 to 1991. More recently he has chaired or co-chaired the Scientific Assessment for the Intergovernmental Panel on Climate Change (IPCC) and, drawing widely on the findings of that panel, has written a definitive account of the science of climate change, published as *Global Warming: The Complete Briefing*.

In 2006 there was a significant and very welcome Declaration from evangelicals in America. The Evangelical Climate Initiative describes itself as a group of senior evangelical leaders in the United States 'who are convinced it is time for our country to help solve the problem of global warming. We seek to do so in a way that creates jobs, cleans up our environment, and enhances national security by reducing our dependence on foreign oil, thereby creating a safe and healthy future for our children. Our deep commitment to Jesus Christ and his commands to love our neighbors, care for "the least of these," and be proper stewards of His creation compels us to act.' Their Statement is called 'Climate Change: An Evangelical Call to Action'.[10]

The Church of England produced its own report, *Sharing God's Planet*,[11] in 2005. This sought to provide a Christian vision for a sustainable future, developing a constructive biblical and theological perspective on the world made by God and as an expression of God's love, and on humanity as God's stewards, prophets, priests, and kings under God's sovereignty. The Church of England has attempted to put its own house in order by launching a 'Shrinking the Footprint' campaign, asking each church in the country to make an assessment of energy use in all church-owned buildings, and work towards signifi-

---

10 For more information, see www.christiansandclimate.org and the link to 'Statements'.

11 A Report from the Mission and Public Affairs Council of the Church of England, 2005.

cant reductions. More recently, *How Many Lightbulbs Does it Take to Change a Christian?*[12] provides practical help towards developing a Christian lifestyle and shrinking the ecological footprint. Among the huge volume of publications on the environment from Christian sources in recent years, I believe one deserves particular mention. The Report of the 1998 Lambeth Conference of Anglican bishops has become best known for its Resolution 1.10 on Human Sexuality. The excessive concentration on that Resolution has clouded the fact that there are other Resolutions, notably 1.8 on Creation and 1.9 on Ecology. Resolution 1.8 is worth quoting in full:

This Conference
(a) reaffirms the Biblical vision of Creation according to which: Creation is a web of interdependent relationships bound together in the Covenant which God the Holy Trinity has established with the whole earth and every living being.
(i) the divine Spirit is sacramentally present in Creation, which is therefore to be treated with reverence, respect and gratitude;
(ii) human beings are both co-partners with the rest of Creation and living bridges between heaven and earth, with responsibility to make personal and corporate sacrifices for the common good of all Creation;
(iii) the redemptive purpose of God in Jesus Christ extends to the whole of Creation.

(b) recognises:
(i) that unless human beings take responsibility for caring for the earth, the consequences will be catastrophic because of:
- overpopulation
- unsustainable levels of consumption by the rich
- poor quality and shortage of water
- air pollution
- eroded and impoverished soil

---

12 Claire Foster and David Shreeve, *How Many Lightbulbs Does it Take to Change a Christian?*, 2007.

- forest destruction
- plant and animal extinction;

(ii) that the loss of natural habitats is a direct cause of genocide among millions of indigenous peoples and is causing the extinction of thousands of plant and animal species. Unbridled capitalism, selfishness and greed cannot continue to be allowed to pollute, exploit and destroy what remains of the earth's indigenous habitats;

(iii) that the future of human beings and all life on earth hangs in a balance as a consequence of the present unjust economic structures, the injustice existing between the rich and the poor, the continuing exploitation of the natural environment and the threat of nuclear self-destruction;

(iv) that the servant-hood to God's creation is becoming the most important responsibility facing humankind and that we should work together with people of all faiths in the implementation of our responsibilities;

(v) that we as Christians have a God-given mandate to care for, look after and protect God's creation.

(c) prays in the Spirit of Jesus Christ:
(i) for widespread conversion and spiritual renewal in order that human beings will be restored to a relationship of harmony with the rest of Creation and that this relationship may be informed by the principles of justice and the integrity of every living being, so that self-centred greed is overcome; and
(ii) for the recovery of the Sabbath principle, as part of the redemption of time and the restoration of the divinely intended rhythms of life.

Resolution 1.9 on Ecology then includes a call to ecumenical partners and other faith communities, governments and transnational companies to work for sustainable society in a sustainable world; to recognize the dignity and rights of all people and the sanctity of all life, especially the rights of future generations; to ensure the responsible use and re-cycling of natural resources; to bring about economic reforms which will establish a just and fair trading system both for people and for the environment.

That was in 1998. It was urgent enough then. Since then the Intergovernmental Panel on Climate Change, drawing together about 300 climate scientists[13] from around the world, has made its significant reports, the scientific consensus on climate change and its likely effects has become much firmer, and the world has become more aware of what the Lambeth bishops called the 'catastrophic' consequences of inaction. Here is a summary of what some of these include.

What the experts say

The energy from the sun comes into our atmosphere as electro-magnetic radiation. Some of it warms the earth's surface. Some is radiated back as infra-red radiation into space through the atmosphere, and this serves to cool the earth. Some of this outgoing radiation is absorbed by the atmosphere, and heat is 'trapped'. The thicker the atmosphere the more heat is trapped, and the more the earth's surface warms up. This is a natural 'greenhouse effect', and is caused by the presence of 'greenhouse gases' such as water vapour, carbon dioxide, methane and ozone in the atmosphere. Some gases, such as carbon dioxide, very strongly absorb heat. Others, such as nitrogen, even though present in much larger quantities, do not. There needs to be a balance between incoming and outgoing radiation for the earth's average surface temperature to remain such that human life is possible (around 14 deg.C). This level of 'global warming' is healthy and positive. If the earth had a much thinner atmosphere it might be more like Mars where the temperature reaches an average of 37 deg.C in the daytime, but

---

13 There were about 300 climate scientists who authored the Working Group on science, but then about 500 environmental and social scientists (not climate experts) drafted the report from Working Group 2, and about 500 economists, engineers and social scientists who drafted the report from Working Group 3. Hundreds of others, expert in different disciplines, offered review comments.

falls to −120 deg.C at night, and on which life as we know it would be impossible.

However, an increase in the amount of greenhouse gases in the earth's atmosphere leads to an increase in the amount of radiation absorbed, and so more heat is trapped. The vast majority of scientists agree that the earth's surface is heating up. There has been some dispute as to the extent to which this is due to human activity (anthropogenic), and how much is the natural cycle of temperature change with the earth experiencing warmer or colder periods across the centuries. There have been ice ages; there have been some warmer periods. However, the increase in the earth's average temperature of 0.75 deg.C since the industrial revolution and particularly in the last 40 years, is much larger than anything that has happened in at least 2,000 years. By looking at gases trapped in cores of ice from the Russian Vostok station in Antarctica, scientists have found that atmospheric carbon dioxide is now at a 35% higher level than it has been for the past 400,000 years, over four ice-age cycles.[14] Methane is up by 50%, nitrous oxide by 15%, and there are some new 'greenhouse gases' such as chlorofluorocarbons which did not exist in the atmosphere before industrialization. A huge majority of scientists now agree that human action has been a strong contributor to global warming through such activities as the burning of fossil fuels and the destruction of the world's forests.

The report of a working group of the Fourth Assessment Report for the Intergovernmental Panel on Climate Change (2007) summarized the findings of a significant group of world scientists:

> Global atmospheric concentrations of carbon dioxide, methane and nitrous oxide have increased markedly as a result of human activities since 1750 and now far exceed pre-industrial values determined from ice cores spanning many

---

[14] Houghton, *Global Warming*, pp. 67f., and referred to in The Royal Commission on Environmental Pollution 22nd Report: *Energy: The Changing Climate*, Crown Copyright 2000, p. 22.

thousands of years . . . The global increase in carbon dioxide concentration is due primarily to fossil fuel use and land use changes, while those of methane and nitrous oxide are primarily due to agriculture . . .[15]

In *Global Warming*, John Houghton presents an estimate that, in the absence of efforts to curb the rise in emissions of carbon dioxide, the global average temperature will rise by about a third of a degree Celsius every ten years, or about three degrees in a century.

> This may not sound very much . . . but it is not the temperature at one place but the temperature averaged over the whole globe. The predicted rate of change of three degrees a century is probably faster than the global average temperature has changed at any time over the past ten thousand years. And as there is a difference in global average temperature of only about five or six degrees between the coldest part of an ice age and the warm periods in between ice ages . . . we can see that a few degrees in this global average can represent a big change in climate. It is to this change, and especially to this very rapid rate of change that many ecosystems and human communities (especially those in developing countries) will find it difficult to adapt.[16]

Houghton says that 'Carbon dioxide provides the largest single contributor to anthropogenic radiative forcing'[17] (that is, the human-induced change in average net radiation at the top of the lower atmosphere because of a change in greenhouse gas concentrations).

Of course, predictions for future climate scenarios depend on a lot of assumptions, and Houghton lists population growth, economic growth, energy use, the development of energy sources

---

15 Working Group 1 contribution to the Fourth Assessment Report of the Intergovernmental Panel on Climate Change, *Climate Change 2007: The Physical Science Basis*, p. 2, 'Summary for Policymakers'.
16 Houghton, *Global Warming*, p. 10.
17 Houghton, *Global Warming*, p. 39.

and the influence of demands to preserve the environment as likely significant factors.[18] But whereas variations in atmospheric carbon dioxide concentration have varied between about 200 and 280 parts per million over the past 160,000 years, until the time of the industrial revolution, from about 1750 AD onwards the concentration has been rising steeply, and is now about 380 parts per million – that is 35% higher. If we continue as we are with no attempt to curb greenhouse gas emissions, the carbon dioxide concentration is predicted to rise to between 480 and 650 parts per million by the end of this century.[19] These rises in levels of carbon dioxide in the atmosphere correspond to rises in the average temperature of the earth. So since the industrial revolution, the earth's average temperature has already risen 0.75 deg.C. It takes a long time for the warming effects of carbon dioxide in the atmosphere to raise the average temperature of the earth, and it has been calculated that even if no more carbon dioxide is emitted into the atmosphere, it is very likely that the earth's average surface temperature will in any case rise another 0.5 degree or so, bringing the temperature to 1.25 deg.C above pre-industrial levels. However, if we do carry on emitting carbon at the same rate as now, by the end of this century the global average temperature is predicted to rise by between a further 1.1 deg. and 6.4 deg.C. The upper half of this range would represent the fastest change in the earth's temperature for at least the past 10,000 years.

Of course, there are uncertainties in any scientific predictions, but it was partly to achieve the best assessment of present knowledge that the Intergovernmental Panel on Climate Change was set up. In its Fourth Assessment Report of 2007, the authors state: 'The understanding of anthropogenic warming and cooling influences on climate has improved since the TAR [Third Assessment Report], leading to *very high confidence* that the global average net effect of human activities since 1750 ... and its rate of increase during the industrial era is *very*

---

18 Houghton, *Global Warming*, p. 41.
19 Houghton, *Global Warming*, p. 69.

GLOBAL WARMING

likely to have been unprecedented in more than 10,000 years.'[20]

The authors of this Report are clear that warming of the climate system is now unequivocal,[21] and numerous long-term changes in climate have been observed, such as changes in Arctic temperatures and ice, ocean acidity, and aspects of extreme weather including droughts, heavy precipitation, heat waves and the intensity of tropical cyclones.[22] The last time the polar regions were significantly warmer than the present for an extended period (about 125,000 years ago), reductions in polar ice volume led to the global sea-level being between 4 and 6 metres higher than today, and many places that are now land were then under water.[23]

The *National Geographic Magazine* published a supplement in October 2007, setting out a helpful summary of the findings from the experts on what might be expected to happen to the earth as its average global temperature rises. Though a few regions such as parts of Russia and northern Europe could benefit from warmer years, most of the world will suffer, particularly the tropics and poorer nations without the economic resources to adapt.

For up to another 2 deg. C rise in earth's average temperature, they predict:

- increasing rainfall in many areas, leading to more frequent flooding
- increasing drought and declining water supply in other areas
- hundreds of millions of people will face increasing risk of water shortages, due to decreased river run-off and loss of glaciers
- though cereal crop yields might improve in some latitudes, they would decrease in other latitudes

---

20 IPCC Fourth Assessment Report, 'Summary for Policymakers', p. 3. (*Very high confidence* represents at least 9 out of 10 chance of being correct; *very likely* means a greater than 90% probability of occurrence.)
21 IPCC Fourth Assessment Report, 'Summary for Policymakers', p. 4.
22 IPCC Fourth Assessment Report, 'Summary for Policymakers', p. 5.
23 IPCC Fourth Assessment Report, 'Summary for Policymakers', p. 8.

- increasing illness and death from heat, storms, floods, droughts and fires and a rise in malnutrition
- a changing distribution of insects reaching new areas with malaria and dengue, though cold-weather-related deaths will decline
- storms and rising sea levels will cause growing erosion of coasts
- many plants and animals will be pushed to higher latitudes; corals would begin to die and the oceans become more acidic.

Between 2 degrees and 4 degrees rise:

- health services would be substantially strained
- coastal flooding would affect millions of people and a significant proportion of coastal wetlands would be lost
- coral reefs would die
- ecosystems would become sources of more carbon as permafrost thaws or vegetation burns or decays.

Above 4 degrees rise it is predicted:

- cereal crop yields would decrease across all latitudes
- more than 40% of the earth's species would face extinction.

The authors do not explore very fully what might happen if temperatures were to rise by, say, 5 degrees. Beyond this level of warming, the risks of major and irreversible changes in the climate system become much greater, although scientists only have tentative ideas about what these may be. If the ice shelves of Greenland or Antarctica were to melt, not only would sea levels rise significantly, threatening many of our coastal cities as well as low lying islands, but also the change in the salt concentration of the oceans could itself affect global weather patterns, for example by changing the Gulf Stream which has such a profoundly positive effect on the weather of the UK. If the Siberian permafrost were significantly to melt, it is difficult to predict what effect the release of large quantities of methane would have. If the Arctic ice were to disappear – as seems increasingly likely – with its capacity to reflect some of the sun's heat back from the earth, not only would Arctic polar bears and walruses become extinct, but the Arctic itself would become a heat-sink rather than a heat-reflector, and the rate of warming would increase.

Catastrophe

If no steps are taken to curb carbon emissions, and the earth's temperature continues to rise, a point could be reached – a few scientists say it may be reached when temperatures rise above another 1.3 deg.C from today – when the situation becomes unpredictable and unmanageable. This is approaching what the Lambeth bishops called 'catastrophic'. Some writers, such as James Lovelock,[24] believe that we may have reached that point already. Others think there is still just about time to do something about it. If a certain temperature is reached, there could be a series of possible positive 'feed-back' loops, whereby the more the temperature rises, the more carbon is released, making the process increasingly non-linear, unpredictable and unmanageable. The conclusion some scientists are reaching is that in order to avert catastrophe, there will need to be an average cut in carbon emissions by the year 2030 of around 80–90% in the rich countries such as the UK,[25] France, Germany, Australia, USA and Canada. If this is anywhere near correct, this adds up to an urgent need for human beings to reduce carbon emissions significantly, if likely damaging risks are to be averted. Whatever we do, there will in any case be significantly more global

---

24 James Lovelock, *The Revenge of Gaia*, 2006.
25 The British Prime Minister Gordon Brown proposed a UK target of 80% reduction in carbon emissions by 2050. The Defra report 'Climate Change: The UK Programme 2006' suggested a limit of 450ppm or lower, and the Council of the European Union in 2005 concluded that 'reduction pathways by the group of developed countries in the order of 15–30% by 2020 and 60–80% by 2050 compared to the baseline envisaged in the Kyoto Protocol should be considered'.

warming to come because of what we have already done to the planet which will inevitably have some effect on our water supplies, our food, our health, our coastlines and our ecosystems. There may be millions of climate migrants moving to more habitable parts of the world.[26] There may be loss of species of plants and animals.

If we do not act . . .

The 2006 Stern Review Report[27] approached the whole question from the perspective of economics. In it, Sir Nicholas Stern concluded that the economic benefits of early action considerably outweigh the costs. He argued that 'the scientific evidence is now overwhelming: climate change is a serious global threat, and it demands an urgent global response'. The Review estimated that if we don't act, 'the overall costs and risks of climate change will be equivalent to losing at least 5% of global GDP [Gross Domestic Product] each year, now and for ever. If a wider range of risks and impacts is taken into account, the estimates of damage could rise to 20% of GDP or more.[28] In contrast, the costs of action – reducing greenhouse gas emissions to avoid the worst impacts of climate change – can be limited to around 1% of global GDP each year.'

---

26 Recent research from the Tyndall Centre for Climate Change Research indicates that 150 million people could be exposed to a '1 in 100' year coastal flood event by 2070, up from 40 million today. The estimated financial impact of such an event would also rise to US$35 trillion by 2070, up from US$400 billion today. The study analyses the exposure of people and property and infrastructure to a 1-in-100 year flood event.

27 Sir Nicholas Stern, *The Stern Review Report to H M Treasury*, 2006.

28 Stern is assuming that we will all be between two and four times wealthier by then, so 20% may not be as large as it appears. To arrive at these conclusions he has made a number of fundamental ethical judgements about the way the world is: the figures do not all arise directly from the science.

In other words, Stern argued, economic self-interest is also served by decisive, urgent action now to combat greenhouse gas emissions. If no action is taken, he argued, the concentration of greenhouse gases in the atmosphere could reach double its pre-industrial level as early as 2035, virtually committing us to a global average temperature rise of over 2 deg.C, and in the longer term committing us to the very dangerous possibility that temperature rise would exceed 5 deg.C. 'Such a radical change in the physical geography of the world must lead to major changes in the human geography – where people live and how they live their lives'.

John Houghton's conclusion also recognizes that the problems are not only global, but also long term. Any programme of action must therefore be 'urgent and evolving, based on the continuing scientific, technical and economic assessments.' He quotes the 1995 IPCC report which states: 'The challenge is not to find the best policy today for the next 100 years, but to select a prudent strategy and to adjust it over time in the light of new information.'[29] How can we reduce and manage climate change without at the same time damaging the proper hopes and ambitions of the poorest societies of the world to move out of poverty and into respect and dignity?

Why should we bother?

This book is written as an answer to that question, but in summary let me say that we should bother because:

- this is God's world, and God has given humanity a responsibility to serve it and protect it
- damage to the planet will cause devastation, harm and death to millions of our fellow human beings
- misuse of the God-given resources of the earth is sin, and left unchecked will cause increasing damage to the earth and to human beings

---

29 Houghton, *Global Warming*, p. 325.

- as Christian people we live in hope that God is redeeming the creation and is calling us now to live in the light of a coming 'new heaven and new earth' marked by justice and righteousness
- global warming is forcing us to face questions about our values, our life styles, our priorities, our hopes and fears, all of which relate directly to the Christian Gospel of God's will for us that his kingdom should come on earth as it is in heaven

We should bother, in other words, because climate change is raising moral and spiritual questions which need urgently to be addressed.

Climate change is real, is growing, and has potentially very dangerous consequences for the well-being of the planet and for human life. I shall argue that a Christian theology of creation celebrates the interconnectedness and interdependence of all creatures within God's cosmic covenant, in which humanity has a significant responsibility to care for and protect the rich variety of species within God's created order. We particularly have a special responsibility for other human beings. The people most affected by climate change will not be in the USA or the UK. They will be living in the poorest and most disadvantaged parts of the world, as indeed they are today.

There is therefore a strong moral imperative towards the planet and towards our fellow human beings to do all we can to avert the danger, reduce the likelihood of global warming continuing at the present rate, and prepare for its likely consequences. This is all about love to our neighbours – both those in disadvantaged parts of the world, and those in generations yet to be born. And, of course, that raises huge questions of priorities. Whose needs come first: the excluded living poor, or people as yet unborn? There is a moral obligation on the present generation not to do things which will significantly damage God's earth, and which will significantly damage the planet's capacity to provide a home for one another now, as well as for our children and grandchildren. There is a further obligation to live within our means. At present rates of energy use and energy consumption, the planet cannot sustain our current way of life – we are running out of earth.

What is global warming changing?

The changing climate is posing questions to humanity which we have not had to face in this way before. It is opening our eyes to the increasing damage we have been causing to the planet (though, of course, in one sense we have been 'damaging the planet' since the Garden of Eden!), especially through Western industrialization and the oil-based economy, of the effects of which for a long time we were not aware.

Rachel Carson's *Silent Spring* woke up many in the Western world in 1962 to the human carelessness, greed and irresponsibility which were having such devastating effects on the rest of the natural order. The indiscriminate use of pesticides such as DDT on insects, weeds and fungi resulted in the death of small rodents, and the huge reduction in the population of some birds – buzzards, for example – because their eggs were poisoned with pesticide. Nature was dying around us because of the 'chemical warfare' being waged for the sake of profit. The birds were ceasing to sing. The spring was silent. Thankfully, since 1962 significant changes in agricultural practices have meant that some threatened species are now recovering in some parts of the world, though 'human carelessness, greed and irresponsibility' are still leading the way in many areas of our planet's life.

If the presenting problems which Rachel Carson addressed have changed in the last 45 years, the fundamental issues have not, and new, urgent questions, particularly concerning energy use and climate change, are now clamouring for a response. As Rachel Carson made clear then, the fundamental problem is one of values – of what value we human beings place on the rest of the natural world, and how we understand ourselves in relation to the rest of creation. In her chapter headed 'And No Birds Sing' she wrote,

Who has made the decision that sets in motion these chains of poisonings, this ever-widening wave of death that spreads out, like ripples when a pebble is dropped into a still pond? Who has placed in one pan of the scales the leaves that might have been eaten by the beetles and in the other the pitiful heaps of many-hued feathers, the lifeless remains of the birds that fell before the unselective bludgeon of insecticidal poisons? Who has decided – who has the *right* to decide – for the countless legions of people who were not consulted that the supreme value is a world without insects, even though it be also a sterile world ungraced by the curving wing of a bird in flight? The decision is that of the authoritarian temporarily entrusted with power; he has made it during a moment of inattention by millions to whom beauty and the ordered world of nature still have a meaning that is deep and imperative.[30]

The Christian faith has a lot to say about values. 'Beauty and the ordered world of nature' are words which correspond readily to those better parts of the Christian traditions which celebrate God's creative love as the source of this world, God's redeeming grace as the heart of this world's hope, and God's Spirit as its life-giving energy. This Trinitarian vision is the basis of Christian values, and gives a meaning to our world 'that is deep and imperative'. Beauty, order and moral imperative will be some of the themes which this book seeks to address. I want to develop the argument that the Christian faith is a major player in human attitudes towards the natural world, acknowledging that by no means have we always got it right, and that sometimes we have been the cause of some of the damage. I believe the Christian Church ought to be more obviously at the forefront of seeking to care for this planet and confront the current ecological issues which threaten disaster. I hope this book might contribute to awakening us further from our present possible 'moment of inattention'. What, then, is global warming changing?

---

30 Rachel Carson, *Silent Spring*, 1962, pp. 118f.

Our human relationship to the planet

In 1967 Professor Lynn White published a now famous paper called 'The Historical Roots of our Ecologic Crisis', in which he argued that the medieval relationship of humanity to the soil, seen in subsistence farming, was profoundly changed by the introduction of power-machine agriculture. There was a shift from a mind-set which saw 'nature' and 'culture' as one entity in their mental and social world, to a mind-set in which 'man' and 'nature' became separate. White blamed the separation of nature and culture on the Judaeo-Christian tradition (and particularly on the teaching about humanity having 'dominion' over the rest of creation), and this has led, he argued, to the destruction of 'nature'.

Regrettably, there have indeed been aspects of the Christian tradition which have contributed not to the healing of this world but to its further destruction. Some approaches to the Bible have led to such a human-centred understanding of the Christian faith that the result has been an exploitation of, rather than a care for and protection of the world around us. Of these aspects of the tradition, the Church needs to repent and change its ways. These were the features of the Christian faith which provoked Lynn White's famous charge that in its Western form, Christianity is 'the most anthropocentric religion' that the world has ever seen, leading to his conclusion that 'we shall continue to have a worsening ecologic crisis until we reject the Christian axiom that nature has no reason for existence save to serve man.'[31] Although White's argument has been criticized on a number of counts by historians and theologians, it is sadly true that some Christians have believed and acted as though nature is only there for us human beings to exploit and use as we wish. This will be discussed further in a later chapter.

At this point we simply need to recognize that we humans, whether we like it or not, are changing the way our earth system

---

31 Lynn White, Jr, 'The Historical Roots of our Ecologic Crisis', lecture delivered on 26 December 1966, Washington DC; repr. in Berry (ed.), *The Care of Creation*, pp. 31ff.

works. Our relationship to the planet is changing. This is to recognize that, as with pesticides in 1962, our actions have consequences, and our actions in human-induced climate change are now contributing to shaping, for good or ill, the world's climate – and therefore everything which depends on it. As Professor Mike Hulme, former Director of the Tyndall Centre for Climate Change Research at the University of East Anglia, has put it: 'Since humans are now an active agent in shaping the climatic future, we have inevitably had to face the question . . . should our climate agency be inadvertent or advertent, purposeless or planned, a mere by-product of our pursuit of tangential individual or collective goals or a consequence of a deliberated and hard-won global strategy? Do we really want to share with nature this burden of climate design?'[32]

In other words, climate change is opening up in fresh and inescapable ways questions about our human relationship to the natural world, our human place in the natural order, the purposes for which we live and act, and the goals for human activity. What is the world for? What are we for? Ultimately, therefore, there is a spiritual dimension to this question which will be explored further in our discussion of creation.

Our attitude to technology

Secondly, climate change forces us to reflect on our human creativity, not least in relation to technology. There are those who see technology as the source of our problems. It is the requirement of energy resources on such a scale, resulting from the industrialization of the world, which has caused the situation in which we find ourselves. There are those who believe that technology can also find us the answer. The Bush administration of the United States seems to hold that belief. Of course, science and technology have brought enormous benefits to the

---

[32] Professor Mike Hulme, 'Setting Goals for Global Climate Governance', unpublished paper, May 2007.

world in the combating of disease, in the easing of life and death, in the production of food, in the possibilities of transport, information sharing, and so on which have so enhanced the lives of so many people. But it is possible to develop a technological mind-set which does not see my relationship to the world around me as a mutual one of partnership, but rather one in which I am set over against the world, able to manipulate it for my own ends. Can the challenge of climate change be answered in terms of human ingenuity and human technical skill? If I see the world only in terms of problems to be solved, and the solution in terms of techniques to be applied, there is an increasing likelihood that the more human and humane styles of relating will be crowded out, and other dimensions – what Carson called beauty, order and moral imperative – will get lost. There will be a loss also of 'the sacred' and in its place will remain an attitude of exploitation and commodification instead of celebration, enjoyment and worship. Climate change is posing these questions to us, and I will take them further in Chapter 4, when discussing the meaning of Sabbath.

The scope of natural justice

A third moral factor which is underlined in a fresh way by climate change is that of natural justice. The fact that the parts of the world most severely affected by global warming will be the places which are most vulnerable, most poor and most disadvantaged is a major moral question put to those of us in the West who have enough. As David Miliband MP said in a speech to the Vatican in May 2007 (when he was the UK's Environment Secretary), this is a moral question. He quoted an address from Pope John Paul II as long ago as 1990 which argued that 'the ecological crisis has assumed such proportions as to be the responsibility of everyone', and went on to say that, 17 years on, the warnings are reaching a crescendo. But he recognized that our call to action must be based on foundations of a new climate-change coalition that go deeper than merely scientific evidence, economic analysis or self-interest. 'They must be grounded in morality and ethics: in a sense of solidarity with the developing world and future generations; a belief that humankind has a duty of stewardship towards nature, and perhaps most critical of all, a belief in securing a socially just balance of responsibility between rich and poor.'

Miliband argued that climate change is not just an environmental or economic issue, it is a moral and ethical one. He said that it is not just an issue for politicians or businesses, but also for the world's faith communities. The World Council of Churches and Christian Aid in their different ways have been right to link issues to do with the environment with issues to do with development in the poorer parts of the world. Climate change is about justice.

Tim Flannery, Director of the South Australian Museum and a Professor at the University of Adelaide, discusses the history of climate change, how it will unfold over the next century, and what we can do about it. His exposition of what might happen leads him straight into questions of natural justice. It is worth repeating the seriousness of the situation:

> Under existing projections, just two countries – Canada and Russia – will reap 90 per cent of the benefit that global warming brings to food crops, while other regions such as Africa and India will lose out heavily with only a small degree of warming. Even conservative studies predict a tripling in the number of humans at risk of food shortage by the 2080s, and such changes may bring issues of natural justice to centre stage in our thinking. Nor will health issues be immune. As our globe warms a degree or two, the percentage of humans exposed to malarial parasites will rise from 45 to 60 per cent. What of those people living in regions marginal for malaria today, who are almost certain to be affected? Add to this the rising seas, changing storm tracks, rainfall and heat waves, and you get a sense of the scope of legal action possible in a world without Acts of God.[33]

---

[33] Tim Flannery, *The Weather Makers*, 2005, p. 288.

GLOBAL WARMING

As Flannery goes on to repeat, any solution will need to be based on principles of natural justice, and if democratic governments do not act voluntarily according to these principles, they may, he says, be forced to do so.

There is a further moral dimension to this in relation to the extent to which poverty is linked to national security. One perspective on this point was provided by Air Chief Marshall Sir John Stirrup, the Chief of the Defence Staff, when he addressed the Royal United Services Institute in December 2006. He was reported to have said:

> Climate change and growing competition for scarce resources are together likely to increase the incidence of humanitarian crises. The spread of desert regions, a scarcity of water, coastal erosion, declining arable land, damage to infrastructure from extreme weather; all this could undermine security. Climate change affects food, health, water, energy infrastructure. Governments are now beginning to treat climate change as a security threat, and has given a new language of 'climate security'.[34] A stable climate is a global public good.

Chapter 5 will pick up the links between development and environmental concerns in an exploration of the meaning of justice.

Questions about energy

Fourthly, climate change is confronting us with questions about health, about food, and most significantly about energy use. Michael Northcott's powerful book *A Moral Climate* argues

---

34 Some of the dangers inherent in using the language of 'climate security' are explored by Professor Mike Hulme in 'Climate Security: The New Determinism', published on the openDemocracy website (www.opendemocracy.net), in which he argues that there is little hard evidence that climate change is a major driver for conflict, and it is dangerous to reduce the complexity of factors in conflict to 'a one-dimensional narrative of cause and effect'.

strongly that at the heart of the global warming crisis there is 'a fundamental conflict between the imperial global economy and the health of the biosphere and its inhabitants', and that accounts of global warming which refuse to recognize this cannot do justice to the real roots of the problem and its solution.[35] The fossil fuel economy, he argues, is 'dangerous to planet earth and to human life, not just because it is warming the climate of the earth but because it is deeply destructive of the diversity and welfare of... ecosystems and human communities.'[36] Northcott likens our reliance on an oil-based economy, and – as he argues – the neo-liberal political theory which underlies it, to the sort of idolatry which led to the exile of the people of God in Jeremiah's day. At the very least, the fact that oil and other fossil-fuel resources are finite and running out faces us with questions about our lifestyles, the choices we make, the priorities we hold, what needs to be preserved and what can be let go for the sake of the health and nourishment of the planet and all its inhabitants. What does neighbour love and natural justice require of Christian people when faced with these questions?

Our vulnerability

A fifth effect is the growing sense of fragility and vulnerability people feel in the face of global warming. The huge loss of life, for example, in the South Asia tsunami in 2004, and in hurricane Katrina in New Orleans in 2005, the prospect of many species becoming extinct and the coral reefs dying, the sense of helplessness in the face of the enormity of the task – all these press on us questions of hope. Can we be optimistic, and on what grounds? If there is a measure of uncertainty and fear in our generation about the likely effects of sea-level rise, and the spectre of severe floods in London, New York, Shanghai and

---

35 Michael S. Northcott, *A Moral Climate*, 2007, p. 269.
36 Northcott, *A Moral Climate*, p. 273.

Calcutta, what vulnerabilities are we creating for future generations? How do we allow future generations to put their needs and their rights in front of us now? Can we be hopeful in the face of the future? And if, as John Houghton argues, 'The biggest challenge the world faces ... is how allowable carbon emissions are to be shared between industrialized nations who have already benefited enormously from cheap fossil fuel energy and developing nations who are determined to grow their economies to a more acceptable level',[37] we wonder whether the human race is capable of such co-operation. Is there not a dimension to the human condition which is ultimately self-centred and self-absorbed, which could frustrate even the best intentions of the best of us to use our creativity positively and for the sake of others? How does the Christian Gospel address questions of human sin and despair? What is God doing in the world? What is God's future for the world? How do Christian people sustain the virtue of hope in the face of moral and spiritual questions such as these?

Thankfully, there has been a responsible tradition of Christian thinking which places a high value on the whole created order as part of the expression of God's creative love, and which looks forward not to annihilation but to transformation. Just as the resurrection of Jesus Christ from the dead gives to Christian believers their hope that, after death, there will be the transformation of their bodies, so the whole created order will, likewise, through death and resurrection, be transformed into the 'new heavens and the new earth' in which God dwells. It is not that heaven is an escape from earth, but that heaven and earth together will be God's home. What this will be we do not know. That this will be is a strong motivation to care responsibly now for the earth on which God has given us life to live and to hope. We need to explore this Christian tradition more fully, as it has to some extent been overshadowed by the ecological movements which took Lynn White's criticisms as reflecting the

---

[37] J. Houghton, from the Foreword to Northcott, *A Moral Climate*, p. vii.

whole Christian story. There is more to tell, and it is hopeful, joyous, full of beauty and full of a 'meaning that is deep and imperative'. It is the basis for a Christian celebration of creation, and the motivation for an urgent Christian ecology.

Climate change is thus opening up for us – in ways which we would not have sought – questions about human life and destiny, about our relationship to the planet and to each other, about altruism and selfishness, about the place of a technological mind-set in our attitude to the world, about our values, hopes and goals, and about our obligations for the present and for the future. These are moral, spiritual and therefore theological questions.

The next five chapters seek to develop a theological vision of the created world and our human place within it. To understand nature as God's creation, to recognize humanity as sharing with the rest of the created order an interdependence of life and food, to discern a source of moral order in the world beyond our personal preferences and tastes which places obligations upon us, to find our human well-being satisfied in terms of global justice, shared resources and mutual support – these theological themes will help us find some markers in the increasingly confusing world we inhabit. The changing climate is changing also the climate of opinion – the way we see ourselves and make decisions about our world. In response to questions posed for us about our relationship to the planet, we need to look again at a theology of creation. Our reflections on technology require us to think again about those other dimensions of life captured by the word 'sacred', and will be explored further in a theology of Sabbath. The questions of natural justice will be explored through what the prophets and Jesus said and did about justice as an expression of neighbour love. Our fears and vulnerabilities can be faced within a theology of redemption and hope.

One central biblical and theological theme in the Judaeo-Christian tradition which holds together many of these values and themes is covenant. It is to a theological exploration of covenant that I now wish to turn.

2

Cosmic Covenant

> Take, eat; this is my body which is given for you . . . Drink this . . . this is my blood of the new covenant which is shed for you.
> Common Worship, Holy Communion

Our theological exploration begins in Jerusalem on Thursday of Passover Week. The year is around AD 30. It is evening, and Jesus is in a large, furnished upper room eating the Passover meal with his twelve disciples. As they were eating he took bread and gave it to them, and then a cup of wine. He gave thanks, gave it to them and they all drank of it. 'This is the blood of the new covenant,' he said, 'which is poured out for many' (see Mark 14.15–25). This simple action which has become the sacrament of Holy Communion within the Christian Church, in response to Jesus' words 'Do this in remembrance of me', holds together many of the themes of this theological exploration.

The Christian Eucharist is a corporate action of communion, of connectedness, of belonging together as the people of God, the Body of Christ. It uses ordinary parts of God's good creation, bread and wine. It is a response of gratitude (eucharist) for God's gift. It is a reminder of God's commandments and the calling to obedience. It resonates with the themes of Passover and Exodus, as it holds before us the death of Christ on the cross, and therefore grace, redemption, and freedom. In a unique way it brings the circle of divine grace and the circle of human need to intersect, bringing heaven and earth together, and catching us up into the sense of wonder at the holiness and graciousness of God. It is both a remembrance of God's gift in the past, and also a hopeful anticipation of God's future. St Paul writes that 'as often as you eat this bread and drink this cup you proclaim the Lord's death until he comes' (1 Cor. 11.26). We are sent out in hope, in the power of the Spirit, 'to live and work to God's praise and glory'. And at the centre of Jesus' inaugural meal in that upper room, he describes what he is doing in terms of 'covenant'.

There is a huge weight of meaning in the word 'covenant' which would not have been lost on the twelve disciples sharing that meal. We shall need to stand back from the immediate questions of climate change for a while to get our bearings.

A new covenant

There are certain computer programs which provide maps of the earth, the different countries, towns and cities within those countries, and even particular streets and buildings, depending on the chosen focus. We need to 'zoom out' from the upper room in Jerusalem – and also, so to speak, 'zoom back' in time – to place Jesus' words about a 'new covenant' in a wider context and a longer timescale. The words 'new covenant' are used by the prophet Jeremiah in the sixth century BC, as he had been grieving over the faithlessness of God's people which had brought upon them God's judgement, and many of their leaders had been taken to exile in Babylon. Jeremiah's message is predominantly gloomy, but it is not without hope. He sees beyond the present pain and uncertainty to a time when God will bring in a new beginning.

> The days are surely coming, says the LORD, when I will make a new covenant with the house of Israel and with the house of Judah . . . I will put my law within them, and I will write it on their hearts; and I will be their God and they shall be my people. (Jer. 31.31f.)

The prophet Ezekiel, who was one of those taken into exile himself, also speaks of a coming time when 'I will make a covenant of peace with them: it shall be an everlasting covenant with them, and I will bless them' (37.26).

Abraham

What is this about? We need now to zoom further out and in time zoom further back to include the story of God's people Israel from its very beginnings centuries earlier than Jeremiah and Ezekiel, to the time of Abraham. For the primary story about 'covenant' in the Hebrew Bible is the story of the covenants made between God and certain individuals who come to represent the people of Israel. We do not need to worry here about the various attempts that have been made to link Israel's covenants with other sorts of treaties made in the Middle East at these times. What we need to know is that essentially a covenant is the establishment of a relationship based on a promise, a relationship that grows over time, and which carries certain obligations. It starts with God's initiative of grace. So in the early story of the patriarch Abraham, God promises that he would be a God to him, and that in Abraham's offspring all the nations of the world would be blessed (Gen. 12.3; 15.8, 18; 17.6–8). God promises that Abraham will be blessed with a family and God promises Abraham a land to live in. The gift of community and the gift of land belong together. The initiative is God's who makes certain promises; it is God who provides the means by which Abraham can fulfil his part of the covenant. It is this formative covenant to which much of what we call the Old Testament, and also much later St Paul in the New Testament, look back, interpreting God's promises to Abraham as the beginning of the story of the people of God, which comes to its climax in 'the new covenant' shared between Jesus and his disciples in the upper room on the night on which he was betrayed.

The covenant with Abraham is depicted as a response to what has gone wrong in creation as depicted in the first 11 chapters of the book of Genesis. In the earlier chapters before chapter 12 when Abraham appears, we have read about God's creative work, about God's man and woman in God's garden, about sin and judgement, and the growth of human wickedness and of people trying to live as though they were God. We have read of the judgement of Noah's flood and God's promise of renewal. We have learned of the arrogance of the people trying to build the tower of Babel and the scattering of the nations in confusion and disintegration. There is a pattern through Genesis 1–11 of sin and judgement, then of grace and hope until the end of chapter 11 which leaves us just with God's judgement. When we, the readers, ask 'What now? Are you, Lord, going to leave your people scattered and confused and separated?' then we are ready for chapter 12 and God's promise to build a new community as the family of Abraham – through whom, we are told, all the families of the earth will receive God's blessing (Gen. 12.3). Then we discover that God's blessing to Abraham seems to 'answer' the judgements and curses we have read about through chapters 1–11. The ground was cursed in Genesis 3.17 – Abraham is promised a land to possess (15.7). Cain was cursed and became a wanderer (4.11, 12); Abraham the wanderer is given a home. Cain, and the Nephilim and the builders of Babel all sought to make a name for themselves; God says to Abraham, 'I will make your name great' (12.2). The families of the nations are scattered at Babel; in Abraham all the families of the earth will be blessed (12.3).[1] God's covenant with Abraham is about land, about community, about blessing (Gen. 17.1–8). It can be focused in a phrase which is frequently used throughout the story of God's covenants with his people: 'I will be your God; you will be my people'.

Moses

The theme of God's covenant with his people comes back later in the story of the Exodus centring on the prophet and leader Moses. This is a covenant made with the whole people of Israel,

---

[1] Cf. David Atkinson, *The Message of Genesis 1–11*, 1990.

starting again with God's initiative of grace, this time in rescuing his people from slavery in Egypt on Passover night (Exod. 12). Again, though with different emphases, it concerns God's promise, and is very clearly understood to be a fulfilment of the covenant with Abraham (Exod. 2.24). With Moses the central focus is on the giving of *torah* – instruction from God to govern the life of the people he has rescued and redeemed. The heart of this is what has come to be called 'The Book of the Covenant', which includes the Ten Commandments and other laws concerning the life of the people of that time. The obligations of the covenant are spelled out in different ways. One is the so-called Holiness Code of Leviticus, which seems to revolve around the central word which is picked up by Jesus in the New Testament: 'You shall love your neighbour as yourself' (Lev. 19.18). That love is expressed in holiness: 'You shall be holy as I the LORD your God am holy' (Lev. 19.2). It is also expressed in justice. 'You shall not render an unjust judgement, you shall not be partial to the poor or defer to the great; with justice you shall judge your neighbour' (Lev. 19.15). As Walter Brueggemann puts it, 'the whole is arranged to show that the *love of neighbour* has become the key component of a vision of holiness'.[2] And, further, that neighbour love develops the meaning of holiness to include the ethical aspect of justice. In summary: in the covenant with Moses, God's blessings follow obedience to God's ways; judgement is the result of disobedience. God's covenant promise expects a response of love, the social dimension to which is justice.

David

It is the covenant of Moses' time which is then ratified in the story of Joshua. 'The people said to Joshua, "The LORD our God we will serve and him we will obey"' (Josh. 24.24f.). The

---

2 W. Brueggemann, *An Introduction to the Old Testament*, 2003, pp. 72–3, quoting Mary Douglas, 'Justice as the Cornerstone: An Interpretation of Leviticus 18–20', *Interpretation* 53 (1999), pp. 341–50.

covenant theme then comes back later in the narratives concerning King David, whose kingdom becomes seen as the fulfilment of God's promise to Abraham, as well as David the king pointing forward to God's coming Messiah, another theme which, according to the New Testament, comes to its climax in the kingly rule of the Lord Jesus. So Psalm 89 refers to God's covenant with his chosen one, and Psalm 132.11–18 reinforces the divine initiative, the divine blessings and the expectation of obedient holiness. When, later, the prophet Jeremiah looks forward, as we have seen, in hope to God's promised future, and he uses the language of 'new covenant', the sense is of God's covenant promises to Israel (Abraham, Moses, David), being renewed and reformulated, reshaped and re-energized.

The book of Deuteronomy: blessing the land

The book of Deuteronomy – which, whatever its precise date, came to prominence at the time of the good reforming King Josiah, a contemporary of Jeremiah – is essentially a book about God's covenant. It is rooted in the loving faithfulness of God: 'Know, therefore, that the LORD your God is God, the faithful God who maintains covenant loyalty with those who love him and keep his commandments' (7.9). And for God's people who obey his laws and statutes, and who live in his ways, they will find that this makes for the best for human flourishing ('You must follow exactly the path that the LORD your God has commanded you, so that you may live and that it may go well with you'; 5.33). They will also enjoy God's blessing. And for the covenant of God with his people Israel, that blessing is also a blessing of the land.

> The LORD your God is bringing you into a good land, a land with flowing streams, with springs and underground waters welling up in valleys and hills, a land of wheat and barley, of vines and fig trees and pomegranates, a land of olive trees and

honey, a land where you may eat bread without scarcity, where you will lack nothing, a land whose stones are iron and from whose hills you may mine copper. You shall eat your fill and bless the LORD your God for the good land that he has given you. (Deut. 8.7–10)

The land, then, becomes a symbol of God's covenanted blessing. God's gift of land, to be well and appropriately used, is part of God's purpose for his people. It is a 'land that the LORD your God looks after' (Deut. 11.12).

In Deuteronomy, part of the covenant obligation on God's people is to 'live justly': 'Justice, and only justice, you shall pursue, so that you may live and occupy the land that the LORD your God is giving you' (16.20). Some of the regulations particularly reflect what has often been called God's 'bias to the poor': 'When you reap your harvest in your field and forget a sheaf in the field, you shall not go back to get it; it shall be left for the alien, the orphan and the widow, so that the LORD your God may bless you in all your undertakings' (24.19).

Faithful obedience to God's ways brings blessing to people and to the land. But, on the other hand, Deuteronomy makes very clear that abandonment of God's will and God's ways, and a failure to live justly, will result in God's curse – a curse which extends to the cities and the fields and to the fruit of the ground, and in which the climate, too, is affected, with fiery heat and drought and rain becoming dust (28.20f.).

We need to be careful here that we do not build an inappropriate picture of God's judgement and God's action in the world. The danger is to interpret such texts as suggesting that God intervenes in particular ways in the world in response to particular sins. But that is a view that Jesus himself rejects. The tower of Siloam did not kill 18 people because they were worse sinners than anyone else. The suffering man was not blind because of his sins or his parents' sins (Luke 13.4; John 9.3). The point is that God's world is so made that human actions have their effects, that sinfulness has repercussions way beyond the person concerned. Obedience to God's will and God's ways makes for the best for the flourishing of humanity and of the whole created order, but disobedience to God's ways leads to the experience of what Deuteronomy calls God's judgement. There is, in other words, an interconnectedness between human behaviour and the well-being of the rest of creation.

We are talking about a theology of relatedness which begins in God's promise of grace and blessing, which includes a calling to holiness and obedience most clearly understood in terms of neighbour love and the quest for justice in human affairs, with special concern for the poor and disadvantaged, and which carries a note of judgement when God's people go astray.

Covenant as loving generosity

The Deuteronomic historian makes very clear that the heart of God's covenant with his people is love, and it is from God's love that the generous gift of land is made. So in a remarkable paragraph he writes:

> It was not because you were more numerous than any other people that the LORD set his heart on you and chose you . . . It was because the LORD loved you and kept the oath that he swore to your ancestors, that the LORD has brought you out with a mighty hand and redeemed you. Know therefore that the LORD your God is God, the faithful God who maintains covenant loyalty with those who love him. (Deut. 7.7f.)

It was the prophet Hosea, writing in the eighth century in the northern Kingdom of Israel, who more clearly than any linked God's covenant faithfulness to his steadfast, faithful love. The prophet is told to love his adulterous wife, 'just as the LORD loves the people of Israel, though they turn to other gods' (Hos. 3.1). This is love persisting 'in spite of' Israel's unfaithfulness. God's love (Hebrew, *chesed*) is expressed as that of a parent for a wayward child:

> When Israel was a child, I loved him, and out of Egypt I called my son. The more I called them, the more they went from me ... Yet it was I who taught Ephraim [Israel] to walk, I took them up in my arms; but they did not know that I healed them. I led them with cords of human kindness, with bands of love. I was to them like those who lift infants to their cheeks. I bent down to them and fed them. (Hos. 11.1f.)

> I will heal their disloyalty; I will love them freely. (Hos. 14.4)

And it is out of divine love that the gift of land is given to Israel, a gift which honours the covenant promise made long before: 'When the LORD your God has brought you into the land that he swore to your ancestors, to Abraham, to Isaac, and to Jacob to give you ...' (Deut. 6.10). The land is God's gift, flowing from his faithful, covenanted and generous love, the sort of love (*hesed*) which creates and sustains a relationship.

And it is faithful and generous love which is the appropriate response of God's people within God's covenant. Although the text often uses the word 'obedience', the danger for modern readers is that this is interpreted only as an ethic of rules, which can too easily dissolve into legalism. The ethics of the covenant are more personal, and relational, and the word 'allegiance'[3] might carry this sense more fully than simply the word 'obedience'. So Hosea writes of God saying, 'I desire steadfast love and not sacrifice, the knowledge of God rather than burnt-offerings' (Hos. 6.6). And the heart of the obedient response of God's covenant people is to live for God with generous and unselfish lives: 'You shall love the LORD your God with all your heart and with all your soul and with all your might' (Deut. 6.5).

And from the Holiness Code: 'You shall love your neighbour as yourself: I am the LORD' (Lev. 19.18).

---

3 Cf. Helen Oppenheimer, *The Character of Christian Morality*, 1974.

A cosmic covenant

Why are we exploring all this in the context of our concern about climate change? Because behind all these specific covenants, the Bible refers to another, deeper covenant of God with the whole of creation.[4] If we allow our zoom lens to move out to its widest extent, and zoom back in time as far as we can go, we find that the Bible speaks of a covenant of God made with the whole of creation, with every living creature.

The prophet Hosea refers to the people's waywardness, but of God's persistent faithfulness. And the language he uses has echoes of the ancient story of Noah and the flood: 'I will make for you a covenant on that day with the wild animals, the birds of the air and the creeping things of the ground . . . and I will make you lie down in safety' (Hos. 2.18). There is a similar reference in the prophet of the southern Kingdom of Judah, Isaiah, when he writes at about the same time: 'The earth dries up and withers, the world languishes and withers; the heavens languish together with the earth. The earth lies polluted under its inhabitants; for they have transgressed laws, violated the statutes, broken the everlasting covenant. Therefore a curse devours the earth, and its inhabitants suffer for their guilt' (Isa. 24.4f.). It is even more explicit in the later writings where there is an oracle for the people in exile with a reference to God's 'covenant of peace'.

> This is like the days of Noah to me: Just as I swore that the waters of Noah would never again go over the earth, so I have sworn that I will not be angry with you and will not rebuke you. For the mountains may depart and the hills be removed, but my steadfast love shall not depart from you, and my covenant of peace shall not be removed, says the Lord, who has compassion on you. (Isa. 54.9–10)

---

4 Cf. Robert Murray, *The Cosmic Covenant*, 1992.

And the prophet Jeremiah refers to God's covenant with creation as a reassurance that he will be faithful to his covenant with King David:

> Thus says the LORD: If any of you could break my covenant with the day and my covenant with the night, so that day and night would not come at their appointed time, only then could my covenant with my servant David be broken. (Jer. 33.20–21)

Noah's flood

Behind references to the 'everlasting covenant' and to God's 'covenant of peace' there is often implicit or explicit pointing back to the ancient story of Noah and the flood in Genesis 6–9,[5] a story which begins with the evil and self-centredness of humanity caught up in sin, and with the poignant reference to God's sorrow that he had created humanity at all. These chapters weave together some strands of tradition which celebrate God's sovereign activity in his world with other strands which speak more of God's intimacy with his people – his sorrow about human sin (Gen. 6.6), and his grace towards his covenant partner, Noah (Gen. 6.8). The flood story begins in Genesis 6.5 where the extent of wickedness in the earth causes God such pain. As it develops, it becomes a narrative of grace, seen in both judgement and mercy. Judgement in the destructiveness of the flood; mercy in the ark which saves Noah together with his family and animals. The mix of themes of sovereignty and intimacy, judgement and grace are brought together again in the word covenant. Before the flood, here is God's promise:

> I will establish my covenant with you; and you shall come into the ark, you, your wife, your sons and your sons' wives

---

5 Cf. Atkinson, *The Message of Genesis 1–11*.

with you. And of every living thing of all flesh, you shall bring two of every kind into the ark, to keep them alive with you. (Gen. 6.18)

It is after the devastation of flood – a climate that has become destructive to human and other life – that God makes a promise of life again:

God blessed Noah and his sons and said to them, 'Be fruitful and multiply, and fill the earth. The fear and dread of you shall rest on every animal of the earth, and on every bird of the air, on everything that creeps on the ground, and on all the fish of the sea; into your hand they are delivered . . .' (Gen. 9.1–2)

Here is an unmistakeable echo of the creation narrative of Genesis 1. Yet there is a difference. 'Be fruitful and multiply' is a task given to humanity who bear God's image – and the promise to Noah is therefore of a new creation, creation beginning again. But this time there is reference to 'fear and dread' – this is no longer the creation of which it was said, 'This is good'; there is an ambiguity to this new creation which still bears the marks of sin, of brokenness, of judgement. The Noah story also reflects the transition from vegetarian food to animal food – it was significant because it involved the killing of living beings.

And at the end of the story, we read again of the covenant. As 'God remembered Noah', after the waters subsided, the fountains of the deep and the windows of heaven were closed, and it stopped raining, God speaks a covenant word of blessing, the provision of a guiding instruction and law, and the reassurance of the sign of the rainbow:

Then God said to Noah and to his sons with him, 'As for me, I am establishing my covenant with you and your descendants after you, and with every living creature that is with you . . . I establish my covenant with you, that never again shall all flesh be cut off by the waters of a flood, and never again shall there be a flood to destroy the earth.' God said, 'This is the sign of the covenant that I make between me and you and every living creature that is with you, for all future generations. I have set my bow in the clouds, and it shall be a sign of the covenant between me and the earth.' (Gen. 9.8ff.)

In all the darkness of climate catastrophe, the rainbow shines as a sign that God has 'hung up his bow'; God will not repeat the destructiveness of flood; those hostilities are at an end. The bow is a reminder of God's promise, a sign of hope, and a call again to covenant faithfulness and allegiance.

As Jurgen Moltmann put it in a sermon called 'Surviving with Noah',

> The promise never again to destroy all flesh because of its wickedness is an unconditional promise on God's part. It is God's indestructible 'Yes' to his creation. The history of nature, with its changes and chances, and the uncertain history of humanity, both rest on the foundation of God's unconditional will. Natural catastrophes and the human catastrophes of history cannot annul this divine 'Yes' to creation and to the human person. Not even human wickedness can thwart the creator's will towards his creation. God remains true to the earth, for God remains true to himself... Reality in its deepest foundations is worthy of trust, for it is good. In the abyss of our disappointments we find God's grace. In the bitterness of suffering that offers no escape we find God's love. At the heart of everything is God's unswerving 'Yes'. And God stands firm.[6]

God's promise, symbolized in the rainbow, therefore is God's covenanted commitment to his creation. This is God's world, and ultimately and despite all appearances sometimes, it is in his hands. As the psalmist put it, 'The earth is the Lord's and all that is in it, the world and those who live in it' (Ps. 24.1).

---

6 In J. Moltmann, *The Power of the Powerless*, 1981, p. 10.

It was the fourth Gospel in the New Testament which gave us the explicit statement that 'God so loved the world' (John 3.16). On this great text, William Temple commented:

> No object is sufficient for the love of God short of *the world* itself. Christianity is not one more religion of individual salvation, different from its fellows only in offering a different road to that goal. It is the one and only religion of world-redemption. Of course it includes a way of individual salvation . . . But its scope is wider than that – as wide as the love of God.[7]

The cosmic covenant, then, begins in God's love, in his gracious and generous gift. *Creation itself is God's covenanted gift. The cosmic covenant is God's commitment to his creation.* Deriving from God's love, it is God's loving and faithful commitment to its well-being. It centres on God's initiative of grace expressed both in mercy and judgement. It lays obligations on humanity to live obediently in response to God's grace in loving and generous allegiance to the covenant Lord. It indicates the consequences of human self-centredness not being curbed and it holds out the promise of a renewed creation under God's blessing.

Covenants with people and with the earth

We have taken our time looking at the scriptures which refer to God's covenant with his people and God's covenant with the whole created order, precisely because the two belong together. As John Goldingay notes in his commentary on Isaiah 24,[8] Israel's covenant relationship is an application specifically to Israel of God's general covenant to be faithful to the world. God's prior covenant to the whole world undergirds God's

---

7 William Temple, *Readings in St John's Gospel*, 1939.
8 John Goldingay, *New International Biblical Commentary: Isaiah*, 2001, p. 138.

special covenant with Israel. Furthermore, God's covenant with Israel becomes in Isaiah's vision God's covenant with all people. What is a particular concern of God with Israel gradually becomes a universal concern of God with humanity. In Second Isaiah itself we see that universalizing pattern developed. It becomes so much clearer in the New Testament when we find Jesus broadening the meaning of being the people of God to include much more than simply the house of Israel. It is broadened further on the day of Pentecost when, in a reversal of the scattering at the tower of Babel, God's Spirit is poured out on 'all flesh'. What we learn of God's relationship to Israel and to their land illuminates God's relationships to all humanity and to the whole earth.

This is of huge importance. Christopher Wright makes the point clearly by referring to two triangles of relationships.[9] The smaller triangle of relationships is God – Israel – land. That is the story we have explored of Abraham, Moses and David. But this belongs within a much larger triangle of relationships: God – all humanity – the whole earth. That is the cosmic covenant of peace which God makes with all creation. And the significance of this is that what we learn of God's blessing of the land for Israel gives us clues as to God's blessing of the earth. What we learn of the call to allegiance of the people of Israel illustrates the call to allegiance of the whole of humanity under God. What we see of Israel's responsibility towards its land gives us pointers to humanity's responsibilities for the care of the earth. And, as I shall argue more fully in the next chapter, the essentially personal and relational dimensions to covenant give us a basis for seeing the interdependence and interconnectedness of all things within the created order of God's world.

God's covenanted commitment to his world is therefore the scriptural backdrop to our human engagement with God's creation – and therefore our Christian response to the questions posed for us by our changing climate. Behind all the personal covenants human beings make with each other, lies the personal

---

9 C. J. H. Wright, *Living as the People of God*, 1983, p. 89.

covenant that God makes with his people – with all people – and the cosmic covenant that undergirds both. They are rooted in God's love, and expressed as God's generous gift. Our relationships with the world around us, with other creatures, and our response to changing climate, need to be thought through as a response to God's covenanted 'Yes' to his world.

Christianity's critics

We have earlier acknowledged that Christian people have not always understood our human relationship to God's creation in covenantal terms. We have not always rightly understood our human place within the created order. We have not lived in the light of the interdependence and interconnectedness which God's cosmic covenant indicates. I have already noted Lynn White's view that Christianity is the most anthropocentric faith, and that Christians have contributed to the human exploitation of the natural world. I think he is only partially right about that. But White is not a lone voice. In 1974, Arnold Toynbee wrote that

> some of the major maladies of the present-day world – for instance the recklessly extravagant consumption of nature's irreplaceable treasures, and the pollution of those of them that man has not already devoured – can be traced back in the last analysis to a religious cause, and that this cause is the rise of monotheism.[10]

I believe this view is at best one-sided. But other reasons have also been given linking Christian faith with the current ecological crisis.[11] Some people have argued that the Christian empha-

---

10 Arnold Toynbee, 'The Religious Background of the Present Environmental Crisis', in David and Eileen Spring (eds), *Ecology and Religion in History*, 1974, quoted in Steven Bouma-Prediger, *The Greening of Theology*, 1995, p. 2.
11 Bouma-Prediger, *The Greening of Theology*.

sis on a dualism of soul and body has led to a rejection of the material world, a split between sacred and secular, a denigration of the earth and therefore its misuse and exploitation. Other critics (rightly) link the Christian faith with the viability of modern science in seventeenth-century Europe, but then blame modern science and technology for causing the environmental crisis. Yet others believe that Christians are so heavenly minded, looking for God's new world to be born, that they have little interest or care for the present world. Although that may be true of some versions of Christian eschatology, I shall argue that it misunderstands the biblical witness concerning creation understood as the context for and framework of covenant. It is that *linking* of covenant and creation that we need to get right.

Covenant and creation

Karl Barth's *Church Dogmatics* is written around several major themes, one of which is that 'covenant is the internal meaning of creation, and creation is the external framework for covenant'.[12] In other words, the covenant of God with his people, especially in the narrative which begins with Abraham, answers to the meaning of what it is to be human – what it is to be created by God and in his image. Furthermore, the covenant of God's grace in mercy and in judgement is God's response to the needs of his created world once it has become broken by sin and selfishness. On the other hand, the doctrine of creation gives a framework with a beginning and an ending, which gives a context within which covenant has meaning. There is a deep interconnectedness between God, creation and humanity which is captured by the word covenant. As N.T. Wright put it:

> God called Abraham to solve the problem of evil, the problem of Adam, the problem of the world . . . Israel's calling is to hold fast by the covenant. Through Israel, God will

---

[12] K. Barth, *Church Dogmatics*, III.1, 1945 (ET 1958), pp. 94, 228.

address and solve the problems of the world, bringing justice and salvation to the ends of the earth – though quite how this will happen remains, even in Isaiah, more than a little mysterious. But, second, creation is invoked to solve the problems within the covenant. When Israel is in trouble . . . the people cry to the covenant God precisely as the creator.[13]

As Barth goes on to expound, the relationship between creation and covenant comes to its climax in the incarnation of Jesus Christ. There is a deep interconnectedness between God, creation and humanity, captured by the word 'covenant', which find their focus and meaning in the Jesus who, in the upper room, gave his disciples the 'cup of the new covenant'.

It was as the covenant people of God reflected on their situation, particularly at the time of the exile in the sixth century BC, that their understanding of God as their Creator came to sharper focus as God revealed to them more of what it meant to know him as Creator. If we are to use the concept of covenant to broaden our vision, and to give us a framework for responding to some of the questions posed for us by climate change, it is to a fresh look at the meaning of 'creation' that we now need to give our attention.

---

[13] N.T. Wright, *Creation and Covenant* in *Paul: In Fresh Perspective*, 2005, pp. 21f., commenting on Isa. 51.12f.

3

Creation: the context for covenant

> Blessed are you, Lord God of all creation, through your goodness we have this bread . . . this wine to set before you.
> Common Worship, Holy Communion

Seeing nature as creation

Nothing can prepare you for your first sight of the Grand Canyon. Its awesome immensity, 277 miles long, eight miles wide, one mile deep from the rims down to the Colorado River, quite literally takes the breath away. Visitors are heard to say, 'My God . . . !' in response to their first glimpse of the majestic rock strata stretching out in both directions, to their realization that the small ants they can see crawling in the distance are people on one of the trails, to the occasional sight of a Californian condor soaring across the canyon. The guidebooks speak of the wonder of nature; the Grand Canyon is without doubt one of the wonders of the natural world.

Other experiences of nature also provoke responses of awe and wonder. The beauty of a sunset over a Scottish loch, a starlit sky on a clear night, the myriad coloured fish of a tropical sea. 'Nature' can evoke in us an appreciation of beauty, a sense of our smallness and finitude in the light of nature's majesty and grace. Richard Dawkins, that most evangelical of atheists, points, in his various writings, to the sense of wonder which many scientists experience in response to the natural world. In *Unweaving the Rainbow*[1] he rightly argues that science itself,

---

1 Richard Dawkins, *Unweaving the Rainbow*, 1998, p. 39.

properly understood, leads to a sense of wonder and delight. He discusses Keats' view that Newton's physics had 'destroyed all the poetry of the rainbow' but argues instead that science can lead us to the point where 'A Keats and a Newton listening to each other might hear the galaxies sing'.[2] It is the nearest Dawkins allows himself to come to the sense of worship we find in the poetry of the book of Job or in some of the Psalms.

Wordsworth's poetry captures something of nature's beauty with its evocation of spiritual reality:

> For I have learned
> To look on nature, not as in the hour
> Of thoughtless youth, but hearing oftentimes
> The still, sad music of humanity,
> Nor harsh nor grating, though of ample power
> To chasten and subdue. And I have felt
> A presence that disturbs me with the joy
> Of elevated thoughts; a sense sublime
> Of something far more deeply interfused,
> Whose dwelling is the light of setting suns,
> And the round ocean, and the living air,
> And the blue sky, and in the mind of man,
> A motion and a spirit that impels
> All thinking things, all objects of all thought,
> And rolls through all things.[3]

But of course there is also in nature that which is awesomely destructive and damaging. Tsunamis and hurricanes, floods in India and Bangladesh, volcanic eruptions, droughts in East Africa and parts of Australia, ice-storms in America's mid-West. In the Californian firestorms in the canyons above Los Angeles in autumn 2007, fuelled by the fierce Santa Ana winds, people spoke of the 'power of Mother nature'. Then we also remember Tennyson's famous reference to 'nature red in tooth and claw'.

---

2 Dawkins, *Unweaving*, p. 313.
3 Wordsworth, 'Lines written a few miles above Tintern Abbey'.

CREATION: THE CONTEXT FOR COVENANT

Whether through beauty or destructiveness, this way of seeing nature is a common feature of our culture: nature is simply there, apart from any human influence, and nature moves us human beings emotionally by wonder or by horror.

But there are other ways of 'seeing nature'. In *Man and the Natural World*,[4] Keith Thomas illustrates many changes in social attitudes in England from 1500 to 1800 AD, which affected how nature was 'seen'. For many Christian thinkers around the fifteenth and sixteenth centuries, one common emphasis was on the human exploitation of the natural world: it was there for our benefit; it could be subjected to human will; and it could be exploited to meet human need. 'Man's dominion over nature was the self-consciously proclaimed ideal of early modern scientists.'[5] Thomas acknowledges, though, that side by side with this emphasis on humanity's right to exploit 'inferior species' there was also a strong Christian doctrine of human stewardship and responsibility for God's creatures. Over the next 200 years, that second emphasis came more to dominate the theological scene, and social attitudes changed from one of exploitation to one of interdependence. 'In the seventeenth century it became increasingly common to maintain that nature existed for God's glory and that he cared as much for the welfare of plants and animals as for man.'[6] These new social sensibilities were helped along by numerous social changes, for example the development of the biological sciences, the dethronement of humanity from the centre of things through developments in cosmology, the growth of the habit of keeping household pets, changing attitudes to the countryside, and the development of ideas of conservation in response to the growth of urbanization.

Then, in the twentieth century, as Alister McGrath makes clear, there have been many different ways of 'seeing' nature. He suggests that there have been at least four:

---

4 Keith Thomas, *Man and the Natural World*, 1984.
5 Thomas, *Natural World*, p. 29.
6 Thomas, *Natural World*, p. 166.

- nature as a mindless force, causing inconvenience to humanity, and demanding to be tamed
- nature as an open-air gymnasium offering leisure and sports facilities
- nature as a wild kingdom, encouraging scuba-diving, hiking and hunting
- nature as a supply depot, producing minerals, water, food . . .

McGrath's point is that the definition of nature is actually a social construction[7] and involves 'seeing the world in a certain way'.[8] We do not simply see nature, we see nature 'as' something. Many of the different ways in which the word 'nature' is used in the above list are inconsistent with each other. McGrath goes on to argue that the Christian theologian explores another very particular way of 'seeing' nature – namely, seeing nature 'as Creation'.[9] It is that theme – and particularly humanity's role in relation to the rest of the created order – that I will develop further in this chapter. So it is to biblical pictures of 'creation' that I want now to turn.

Biblical pictures of 'creation'

There are various different pictures of creation in the Bible, and they lead to a number of different ways of thinking about the relationship of humanity to the rest of the world. First, there are some texts that give us a picture of harmony and interdependence, and see human beings united with the rest of creation in a wonderful balance. Secondly, other texts paint a picture of the awesomeness of nature as the creation of a majestic God in which human beings are reminded of their smallness, and a creation over which human beings have no control. And thirdly, yet other scriptures give human beings what at least *seems*

---

7 Alister McGrath, *A Scientific Theology*. I. *Nature*, 2001, p. 109.
8 McGrath, *A Scientific Theology*, I, p. 113.
9 McGrath, *A Scientific Theology*, I, p. 133.

like a central role of mastery over the rest of creation, providing (I think wrongly) some basis to the belief that human beings can manipulate other creatures for their benefit.

Harmony and interdependence

What may be one of the earliest written accounts of God's creation of the world is the familiar story of the Garden of Eden in Genesis 2–3. By contrast with Genesis 1 with its picture of the majestic sovereignty of God over creation, Genesis 2–3 give us a more intimate picture of God's garden, which God enjoys walking round at the time of the evening breeze, and of the place of human beings in God's world. We are told of human creatureliness and human limits; of God's requirement of obedience and the reality of human disobedience; we learn of the fragmentation and disorder of a person's relationship to God, to others, to the natural world. Chapters 2 and 3 of Genesis need to be read together, and they provide a picture of ambiguity – there is much about the garden which is joyous, free and fruitful, intimate and life-giving, and then we find that everything is subject to decay, pain, sorrow and death. The universal questions of human existence are touched on in this poignant narrative: we are there in the garden; it is the ambiguity of our lives that is portrayed.

The theme of Genesis 2, before sin enters the story, is the context of human life in relation to the rest of the life of the earth. Humanity is 'of the earth' (2.7); there is an earthiness about our human nature. Human life is of a piece with animal life. 'Adam' is of a piece with '*adama*', meaning 'the ground'. Human life is of the dust, and returns to dust. We then notice that God 'formed man' (2.7). God shaped humanity out of the earth with his own hands. The picture is of the potter moulding the clay, or of the artist creating a picture. There is a bodily nearness of the Creator to the creature. God, so to speak, gets his hands dirty to bring us to life. This implies God's authority over humanity – God shapes us, and we are inescapably God's embodied creatures. Human life is embodied life. And then into his clay model, God breathes life. Life is God's gift, and the psychophysical unity of the product of clay in God's hands and the breath of God's nostrils – that unity we call a human being – is dependent on God for life and breath and all things. Life is not only 'the dust of the ground', it has also the higher level of an organism: 'the breath of life'.

The author of Genesis 2–3 also wishes to stress that God's gift of life in Eden is the source of all life beyond Eden – hence the significance of water. Although elsewhere water can become the symbol for destructive and frightening power – as in the story of the flood – here in God's garden, water is a principle of life, of growth, of refreshment (Gen. 2.10–14). The garden itself is a park of trees into which God put the man he had formed, and into which he introduced cattle and birds and animals of the field. The garden is a place of beauty and nourishment ('pleasant to the sight and good for food', Gen. 2.9), for humanity and for every living creature. It is a place of God's bountiful provision, which pours out to the world around.

To serve and to protect

The garden is also a place of creativity, in which God's man is charged with the responsibility to act in God's place as the parkkeeper. The phrase is 'to till it and to keep it' (2.15). The word 'till' is a common word used of cultivating the soil. It is also used of serving God, and can perhaps here carry the sense of serving the rest of the created order on God's behalf. The word 'keep' is used elsewhere of 'guarding' or 'protecting'. *So the man in God's garden has the responsibility to 'serve and to protect' the rest of the creation on God's behalf.* The other animals are in the garden as companions for the man, although none of them was fitted to be the sort of 'helpmeet' or complementary companion that the story indicates the woman was created to be. The other creatures are depicted as being close to the man in creaturely proximity. 'The animal too is taken from the earth and is incorporated by man into his circle of life as the environment nearest to him.'[10] The process of naming the animals is both a recognition of human authority, but also an illustration of the way humanity is beginning to 'serve and protect' by bringing some order into the confusion around, and the author is suggesting the development of a benign environment in which humanity and animals share God's garden, which then develops in the story of the creation of woman.

Is there just a hint in the language of being taken 'out of dust' that the writer intends us to recall the language of the elevation of someone to royal office? It is in 1 Kings 16.2 that Baasha's enthronement is reported: 'Since I exalted you out of the dust and made you leader over my people.' Behind the creation formula ('The LORD God formed man from the dust of the ground') does there lie a royal formula of enthronement? Is the calling to serve and to protect the creation an example of royal service?[11]

There is an intimacy and friendliness about this ancient text, which bears comparison with the visions of Isaiah chapters 11 and 65 in which creatures and human beings live in harmony with each other in that day when 'the earth is full of the knowledge of the LORD as the waters cover the sea'. The heart of the life of the garden is that humanity is expected to grow up into the knowledge of God on the basis of allegiance to God and in fellowship with the Creator.

A fallen world

All this throws into very sharp relief the other side of the story of the garden which is depicted in Genesis 3. The coming of human sin into the world, as I will explore more fully in Chapter 6, arises from the tempting voice of the serpent, and results in an estrangement between humanity and God, within themselves, between each other, and significantly between humanity

---

10 G. von Rad, *Genesis*, 1956, p. 81.
11 This suggestion is made in an early paper by Walter Brueggemann, *From Dust to Kingship*, 1972.

and the rest of their environment. What is described as 'God's curse' of the ground (see Chapter 6), is God's judgement on human sinfulness, which leads to pain and toil in the place of joyous fruitfulness and creative work.

The vivid picture painted in this old story is of this world now being an ambiguous place. There is much that is beautiful, and much that is destructive. There is creativity and work, harmony and interdependence, but it is universally marred by pain and toil. There is a communion between humanity and the rest of the created order, intended to be 'served and protected' by human hands, but it is spoiled and fractured and symbolized no longer by 'the tree of life', and by being 'pleasant to the sight and good for food', but by 'thorns and thistles', sweat, death and dust. Creation is the context for God's covenanted relationship with his world, with a delegated responsibility to humanity to act on God's behalf, but it is a context which is now ambiguous: beautiful, yet flawed.

Interdependence

The vision of the garden is one of relationship and interdependence. Humanity is part of creation and not outside of 'nature' – because what we regard as 'nature' is part of the covenant between God and creation. That interdependence means that human actions can affect the way the world works: human sin can affect the environment. Human greed, for example, may well be the basic motivation for burning some rain-forests to grow grain for profit, and doing so unbalances the eco-system, leading in places to mud-slides, in others to extinction of some species, quite apart from the loss of the trees with their important role in the carbon cycle. The vision of interdependence is very close to the concepts being discussed in these words in a declaration published by an international group of scientists in 2001:

> The Earth system behaves as a single, self-regulating system, comprised of physical, chemical, biological and human com-

ponents. The interactions and feedbacks between the component parts are complex and exhibit multi-scale temporal and spatial variability.[12]

This is also very close to what James Lovelock callesd 'Gaia', a metaphor for the living earth, named after a Greek goddess. By Gaia, Lovelock means the whole system of interdependent parts of the life of the earth (similar to what some call the 'biosphere'), which sees the world not as a mechanism, but a 'finely balanced relational nexus of life-forms'.[13] Lovelock also argues that the earth, as a self-regulating system, will itself react when human beings misuse and exploit it. This is the passionate plea in Lovelock's latest work in which he argues that our human misuse of the planet, not least in our reliance on a fossil-fuel economy, is provoking the rapidly changing climate and all other changes associated with it. Gaia is having her 'revenge'.[14] As Christians we need both to understand and acknowledge that interdependence, recover a proper understanding of humanity's role under God in caring for the planet, hear the cries of 'Gaia's revenge', but also keep all this within the ultimately hopeful context of the psalmist: 'The earth is the Lord's and all that is in it', and of God's covenanted 'Yes' to the creation.

Awesome distance

There is a very different account of creation at the end of the book of Job. This profound exploration of innocent suffering draws a picture of a man whose whole life falls apart around him. He loses his family, his livelihood, his health and his hope, and whereas others suggest that his sufferings must come from

---

12 Quoted by Crispin Tickell in his Foreword to Lovelock, *The Revenge of Gaia*.
13 Cf. Northcott, *A Moral Climate*, p. 69.
14 Lovelock, *The Revenge of Gaia*.

his sin or his lack of faith, Job maintains his integrity and his innocence. But that makes it harder for his faith. Where is God in all this pain? The drama continues for 37 chapters of relentless agonizing, and rather fruitless suggestions from Job's friends about God's wisdom, justice and goodness. But through all these 37 chapters God does not respond to Job's pleas. Eventually in chapter 38 God responds to Job from the whirlwind, but with no answer to any of his questions. Instead he faces him with the question of whose world this is: 'Where were you when I laid the foundation of the earth?' (Job 38.4).

Where was Job when God determined the measurements of the world, or laid its cornerstone 'when the morning stars sang together and all the heavenly beings shouted for joy'? Who was it that shut in the sea, made the clouds, commanded the morning? Has Job walked in the depths of the sea, or entered the storehouses of the snow? Has he cut a channel for the rain, or bound the constellations together? Can Job send forth lightning, or put wisdom into the human mind? Can he feed the lion, care for the mountain goat, the wild ass, the ox, the ostrich, the horse, the hawk? Even Behemoth (the hippopotamus) and Leviathan (the crocodile), symbols of fear-making monsters, are held within the Creator's hands. So the question to Job is: whose world do you think this is?[15]

As Oliver O'Donovan wrote,

> Job must learn not to think of nature only in relation to his own wants, but to see the irrelevance of those wants to the vast universe of nature. He is to be humbled by a pageant of natural phenomena . . . the scientific wonder of the ancient world, more unforced than our own, makes this proud specimen of our race feel very small. He has no claim to a stable and well-balanced eco-system in the face of a nature so diverse in its teleologies, so indifferent to human concerns.[16]

---

15 Cf. David Atkinson, *The Message of Job*, 1991.
16 O.M.T. O'Donovan, 'Where Were You . . . ?', in Berry (ed.), *The Care of Creation*, pp. 90f.

CREATION: THE CONTEXT FOR COVENANT

This seemingly harsh and unfeeling perspective underlines our human contingency but – as with Job – can lead us to worship. It throws into sharp contrast the current loss of awe, which has so often given way to an exploitative approach to the natural world. O'Donovan goes on to speak of the good news of the Gospel ('do not be anxious'), of the faithfulness of God to his covenant, and of the judgement of God which some biblical writers find in the terrors of nature, but, reflecting on the book of Job, he asks whether we are prepared to hear the voice of the Creator warning and counselling us about our ways. 'If we are in too great a hurry to accept the responsibility for managing things better, we may never hear the question that he is putting to us. Let our first response, like Job's, be to lay our hands on our mouths.'[17]

A perspective such as the book of Job will be needed in the light of natural disasters which confront us with the question of God's purposes in the face of innocent suffering. It is a book not only about the puzzle of suffering, but also about the puzzle of persistent hope in spite of appearances, and of a faith that God can bring a greater good even out of the most devastating pain. Job is brought face to face with what we would call 'natural evils' – the tempests and earthquakes which seem to be the responsibility of the Creator. Struggling towards an answer to this most difficult of questions, John Polkinghorne develops what he calls a 'free-process defence'.

> In his great act of creation I believe that God allows the physical world to be itself, not in Manichaean opposition to him, but in that independence which is Love's gift of freedom to the one beloved. The world is endowed in its fundamental constitution with an anthropic potentiality which makes it capable of fruitful evolution. The exploration and realization of that potentiality is achieved by the universe through the

---

17 O'Donovan, 'Where Were You . . . ?', in Berry (ed.), *The Care of Creation*, p. 93.

continual interplay of chance and necessity within its unfolding process.[18]

The South Asia tsunami, then, was not a vindictive God punishing innocent people. It was the outworking of the physical processes of shifting tectonic plates which is part of the freedom God has given the world to be itself – a freedom which has 'anthropic potentiality' to enable the universe to be capable of being our home; and not ours only, but the home of all living things, a multitude of species of animals and plants which, as Job was to learn, God has provided for.

The sovereign Lord

There is yet a third biblical perspective alongside that of harmony and interdependence, and that of the awesome distance we find in the book of Job. This third perspective comes in the account of creation given to us in Genesis 1. The poem of beauty and grandeur which opens our Bibles is a hymn of praise to the majesty of the Creator. Similar to, but also profoundly different from, other creation narratives from Mesopotamia, Genesis 1 would have provided a very firm rock of stability to the people of God when faced with the miseries of exile in Babylon. They are called back from the lure of other gods, to the worship of the one sovereign, majestic Creator of all, who, in the transcendent freedom of his creative Word, and with the animating breath of his brooding Spirit, is the source of all things, all life, all creatures, all people. 'The world is charged with the grandeur of God.'[19]

God, we are told, created 'the heavens and the earth'. That is a phrase which describes everything that is not God – the whole universe, seen and unseen. Heaven is 'God's place', as the earth is 'humanity's place' – so Genesis is reminding us that creation

---

18 John Polkinghorne, *Science and Providence*, 1989, p. 66.
19 In Gerard Manley Hopkins, *Poems and Prose*, 1953.

CREATION: THE CONTEXT FOR COVENANT

is 'open to God'. The world is not a closed system of natural causes – it is an open system, addressed by God's creative Word, and inspired by God's life-giving Spirit.

We do not need here to rehearse all the rich nuances of this wonderful chapter at the start of our Bibles. Suffice it to say that the evolution of vegetation and all living creatures is described in terms of an emergent creation, in which all things reproduce 'after their kinds'. Ours is not a ready-made world. There is a principle of newness, of creativity built into it. The picture is of an emerging creation. In one of Tintoretto's paintings, birds and sea creatures are depicted as streaming forth from the Creator's hands, and within that stream of life there is creative power. Within each distinctive strand of living creatures, there is the power for new life. The fruits have seeds in them; the swarming life of the waters, the flocks of birds in the sky, the animals on dry land all have the power of reproduction. They are all empowered to hand on the Creator's gift of life. And behind all this the author writes of the energy of the sun, with light for the day and for the night, and gives us that greatest of all understatements: 'He made the stars also' (Gen. 1.16).

Order and contingence

The picture is of an increasingly ordered world. From the 'confused emptiness' (Calvin's phrase for the 'formless void and darkness' of Gen. 1.2) God brings order. A rhythm of six days leading to a seventh shapes God's world in its rich patterns and categories. Light is separated from dark, waters from dry land; animals are grouped 'according to their kinds' – here is a mind not far from the interests of science. The whole enterprise of science rests on the assumption of an ordered world in which pattern can be discovered and categories established. The ordered rationality of the created world, derived from the transcendent rationality of the creative Word, is the basis for scientific exploration and discovery. But this is a *contigent* order. It is not a *necessary* order, such as could be discovered from a philosopher's armchair. Contingence means that it does not have to be the way it is. God could have made it otherwise – and to discover the world we need to get out of our armchairs and into our laboratories. We need to explore.

Many of the unexpected contingencies of the world, and particularly of the climate, also reflect an underlying order and pattern. The *hydrological cycle*, through which water is continually exchanged between the surface of the earth (where most of it is stored in liquid form in the oceans) and the atmosphere (where it can be present as liquid, gas or solid) takes place through evaporation, transpiration from plants and animals, and precipitation as rain or snow. The *carbon cycle* involves the movement of carbon, from its major stores in the oceans and the rocks and plants, to the atmosphere as carbon dioxide through the respiration of animals, and the movement back from the atmosphere to the plants through photosynthesis. The carbon is trapped in the plants, and oxygen – needed for animal life – is given off by the plants. This removal of carbon dioxide from the air by plants and trees is therefore crucial for the sustaining of animal and human life, which makes preventing the destruction of plant life on such a large scale through deforestation such a vital part of renewing the face of the earth and reducing climate change.

Food chains involve the conversion of solar energy into chemical energy in plants which are then eaten by herbivores, which become food for carnivores, which can then become food for other carnivores higher up the chain. Food chains, the hydrological cycle and the carbon cycle are all 'systems' in which all the individual components belong together. There is a rich and wonderful order to our world systems. As we are learning, however, human action can significantly affect the functioning of these systems – sometimes to our advantage, though in climate change with predominantly adverse results.

This is good!

Before there is any talk of sin or death, the Bible speaks about creation's goodness. There is the repeated refrain through

CREATION: THE CONTEXT FOR COVENANT

Genesis 1: 'And God saw that it was good . . . and God saw everything that he had made, and indeed it was very good.' This is the basis for a celebration and enjoyment of God's world, which in some Christian teaching has got lost behind an almost exclusive emphasis on sin. And the goodness of the world, in all the rich variety of its createdness, is as strong a motivation as one could find to limit the exploitation and pollution of the world, and to work tirelessly for creation's health, ecological balance and well-being. It is important to underline the word 'good' before we consider that more difficult word in this chapter about humanity having 'dominion'.

The goodness of the world means that it matters that we are destroying 100 tonnes of ancient plant life, preserved and fossilized for centuries, to create four litres of petrol. It matters that many species are migrating northwards because of global warming, that some butterflies are becoming extinct, that some caterpillars are surviving for shorter times and so some birds are without food. It matters that some species of snails in Lake Tanganyika have lost two-thirds of their habitat in the past two decades because the surface waters have warmed up, nutrients no longer surface, and plankton has significantly declined. It matters that the Antarctic sea ice is melting with the loss of winter food for krill, and some species dependent on krill for food – such as some whales, seals, penguins – may be threatened.[20] It also matters that the Royal Society for the Protection of Birds[21] has created reserves and protected areas which have allowed expansion of the population of, for example, bitterns, marsh harriers, avocets and Dartford warblers; these reserves create space and time for nature to adapt to change. These things matter because this is God's world and it is good, and what we do to it matters.

---

20 Cf. Flannery, *The Weather Makers*, pp. 77, 88, 91, 98.
21 www.rspb.org.uk

'Let us make humanity in our image'

It is within the rich panorama of creation that humanity's own role is defined. Again, this must have been a source of comfort to God's people away in exile: you, too, have a place in God's purposes for the world. Humanity, male and female, is described as being made in God's image. There have been many books written about the meaning of this phrase. Essentially I believe the image is not primarily some capacity which we have, but a relationship which we are given. There is only one human being of whom it was specifically said, 'He is the image of the invisible God' (Col. 1.15), and if we wish to see the true image of God, we see it in Jesus Christ. When St Paul writes of the glory of Christ 'who is the likeness of God', and of our being changed 'into his likeness', he uses the analogy of a mirror. 'We all . . . seeing the glory of the Lord as though reflected in a mirror, are being transformed into the same image from one degree of glory to another' (2 Cor. 3.18). This suggests that we see the divine image, if the mirror is at the right angle – in the right relationship – to its object. To be 'in' or better 'as' the image of God is then about being in a right relationship with God our Creator. True humanness is found in fellowship with God.

Royal service

In the Genesis text, humankind is given 'dominion':

> Then God said, 'Let us make humankind in our image, according to our likeness; and let them have dominion over the fish of the sea, and over the birds of the air, and over the cattle, and over all the wild animals of the earth, and over every creeping thing that creeps upon the earth.' So God created humankind in his image, in the image of God he created them; male and female he created them. God blessed them, and God said to them, 'Be fruitful and multiply and fill the earth and subdue it; and have dominion over the fish of

the sea and over the birds of the air and over every living thing that moves upon the earth.' (Gen. 1.26–28)

We need to spend some time on this text, which has caused so much confusion, and has sometimes been misinterpreted in terms of a charter for exploitation.

The words 'have dominion' mean 'govern, rule' and are usually used of kings ruling – for example, in the case of Solomon's peaceful rule in 1 Kings 4.24. The sense is that Solomon was the leader, but was not exploitative. The word 'subdue' is not used of humans subduing animals, only of the earth, and the thought here is that humanity is to take possession of the earth, to till it and work it (as in Gen. 2; to 'till' means to 'serve'), but as a partner with the rest of the community of creation.

The picture here, then, is of a paradise, once again rather like Isaiah 11, where there is peace between humanity and the animals, and the whole scene incorporating humanity on behalf of God the Creator, exercising the role of a servant-king as a partner within the community of creation – not dominating, but enabling.

Many Christians describe this human calling as one of 'stewardship', which has the merit of emphasizing that our role is exercised 'on behalf of' another, namely God. However, 'stewardship' is never used in the Bible in relation to creation, and it is an ambiguous term with resonances both negatively of mere 'conservation' as well as positively of the recognition of the place of science and technology in the 'management' of creation. Sometimes, though, it is used of human 'control'; sometimes of subservience. If we are going to talk of 'stewardship' we need to take some care in what we mean.

That role of what I have called 'royal service' becomes even clearer when we realize that the whole of Genesis 1 is a poem of six days leading to a seventh. The climax of the chapter is not the creation of humanity, but the gift of the Sabbath. The focus is on the divine rest – and therefore on human worship. Humanity's role in relation to the rest of creation is also a liturgical one – to share in the rhythm of God's creation, and in our worship to give a voice to the silent order of the universe, that it too, with us, may sing the Creator's praise. The servant-king becomes also, therefore, a priest of creation. Humanity's God-given role is so to serve, lead and manage the rest of the created order that each creature may find its own fulfilment within the shared community of God's ordered world.

Psalm 8 significantly fills out the themes of these last paragraphs. God is the Sovereign whose glory is set above the heavens, and the poet wonders what human beings could be that God is mindful of them. 'Yet you have made them a little lower than God, and crowned them with glory and honour. You have given them dominion over the works of your hands.'

Once again we find the language of dominion, but this has to be understood in the context, first, of the humble reverence and wonder with which the psalm begins, and that human dignity finds its value in being God's gift. Then secondly, we read that humanity is 'crowned' with the kingly function commissioned by God, of caring for 'the works of God's hands'. Here is no exploitation and domination. Here, again, is the work of God's royal servant, committed to care.

In fact, as other psalms remind us forcefully, the true 'king' is committed to service, especially to the cause of the poor and needy. Thus, Psalm 72 prays that the king would be given God's justice and righteousness to 'defend the cause of the poor of the people, give deliverance to the needy, and crush the oppressor' (vv.1–4).

If humanity's role is that of royal service, 'to serve and to protect' the rest of the created order, climate change is defining for us ever more sharply 'the poor and needy' of the world, and reminding us that the obligation to care grows more and more on the peoples who have enough.

Humanity as creation's priest

As we have already intimated, we need to see humanity's role in relation to the rest of creation in priestly as well as royal terms.

CREATION: THE CONTEXT FOR COVENANT

In his powerfully argued book *The Rape of Man and Nature*,[22] Philip Sherrard argues that the philosophical ideas which lie behind modern science and technology have resulted in the dehumanizing of humanity and the exploitation of the natural order. It is the loss of what he calls 'the sanctity' of nature through Western Enlightenment thinking and modern science which is at the root of the predicament of the world and of humanity. This may be overstated, and there are many grounds for thanking God for the gifts of science and technology, and for recognizing that they only lead to dehumanization and desacralization when they become our masters and not our servants. But, drawing helpfully on Eastern theology, Sherrard does rightly emphasize humanity's role as priest, and consequently the sacramental nature of creation.

> Man is called upon to mediate between heaven and earth, between God and his creation. But when he closes his consciousness to what is above it, he obstructs that flow through which material things may be saturated by the Spirit, or the Spirit may become incarnate, and the result is a disorder in creation which brutalizes both man and nature. Because it is only through man fulfilling his role as mediator between God and the world that the world itself can fulfil its destiny and be transfigured in the light and presence of God. It is in this sense that man – when he is truly human – is also and above all a priest – the priest of God: he who offers the world to God in his praise and worship and who simultaneously bestows divine love and beauty upon the world.[23]

---

22 Philip Sherrard, *The Rape of Man and Nature*, 1987.
23 Sherrard, *The Rape*, p. 40. From a very different theological standpoint, the same theme of the priestly role of humanity in relation to creation is underlined by Jurgan Moltmann, *God in Creation*, 1985, p. 228.

'From him, and through him, and to him'

If creation is through God's Word, God's Wisdom and God's Spirit, the New Testament tells us that these are attributes of Jesus Christ, the image of God. He is also described as the Word (John 1.1), as God's Wisdom (1 Cor. 1.30), and there is reference to the Spirit of life in Christ Jesus (Rom. 8.2). He is the one through whom 'all things came into being, and without him not one thing came into being. What has come into being in him was life, and the life was the light of all people' (John 1.3–4). St Paul calls him 'the firstborn of all creation; for in him all things in heaven and on earth were created' (Col. 1.15f.), and elsewhere says magisterially, 'From him and through him and to him are all things. To him be glory for ever' (Rom. 11.36). In other words, the New Testament writers came to see Jesus of Nazareth as the incarnation of God, and referred to Christ as the agent of creation – as well, as we shall see, as its Saviour and Redeemer.

In Jesus Christ we see a Servant King, 'who though he was in the form of God . . . emptied himself taking the form of a slave . . . and became obedient to the point of death' (Phil. 2.5f.). He, the Lord and Teacher, is the one who takes a towel and washes his disciples' feet (John 13.14). No exploitative domination in him; rather, a ministry of service. 'You know that among the Gentiles those whom they recognize as their rulers lord it over them . . . but it is not so among you . . . the Son of Man came not to be served but to serve, and to give his life a ransom for many' (Mark 10.41f.).

In Jesus Christ we see God's priest, who ever lives to make intercession – mediating between God and God's creatures (Heb. 7.24f.).

As we shall see more fully in Chapter 6, it is through Jesus Christ the royal servant and priest that the world sees the authentic human being fully in the divine image, and it is through him that God purposes to gather up all things in Christ, things in heaven and things on earth (Eph. 1.10). It is therefore through Christ's body, the Church, that God's purposes are

CREATION: THE CONTEXT FOR COVENANT

now to be made known (Eph. 3.10), and it is the Church which must learn to 'lead a life worthy of the calling' to which it has been called (Eph. 4.1). The Church becomes the vehicle for bearing witness to the royal service and mediating priesthood which God the Creator expects from humanity in the world.

Renewing the face of the earth

I close this chapter with a reflection on one of the great nature poems of the world, Psalm 104, which fills out in fuller colour many of the themes I have already touched on. On the south rim of the Grand Canyon is an artist's studio, on the doorway of which is a small plaque. It is a quotation from Psalm 104: 'Bless the LORD, O my soul. O LORD my God, you are very great.' It is a fitting response of worship to the wonder of the natural world around. In the poem, the psalmist reflects on God's creation, and is able to see its purpose and its beauty pointing beyond himself to God. It is because of his reflective attention that he *sees*. As Elizabeth Barrett Browning put it, in her poem 'Aurora Leigh',

> Earth's crammed with heaven,
> And every common bush afire with God:
> But only he who *sees*, takes off his shoes,
> The rest will sit around it, and pluck blackberries.

The psalmist begins by calling on himself to sing God's praise, 'Bless the LORD, O my soul', and then (vv. 2–4) celebrates the majesty and honour of the Creator. The light is God's garment, God's palace is built on beams standing on the heavenly sea; the clouds are God's chariot, the wind and the lightning are God's ministers. Everything is there for God's own sake. The psalmist then reflects on the creation of the earth, in particular the bounds set to the chaotic flood waters (vv. 5–9), and is moved again to worship. Water is the source of life (vv. 10–18), and the poet then takes us through valleys and streams and mountains, grass, trees, birds nests and rocks; these are the homes for God's creatures, who are not there to serve humanity, but are simply part of God's gift of life.

Time, along with space, is the Creator's gift (vv. 19–23), and the sun, the moon and the seasons are all part of the ordering of the creation. God gives food to the creatures, even the lion's roar is interpreted as a prayer. 'The earth is full of your creatures'; even Leviathan, the monster crocodile, is there as God's playmate. The psalmist reminds us of God's delight. All God's manifest works are made 'in wisdom' (v. 24). They all rely on God's Spirit (v. 30) for their life. Here, in embryo, is a vision of God as Creator, wisdom and giver of life which later Christians have filled out in the doctrine of the Holy Trinity. And all life is preserved and sustained by God who gives food from his open hand (v. 28).

But death, as much as life, is part of God's power: all things come into being and then pass away into dust. God's generous gift of life constantly renews the face of the earth, even in the midst of its dying (v. 30). God does not abandon his creation, but persistently and consistently sustains it and preserves it by his breath of life. As Kidner pertinently comments, 'This, so far from implicating Him in our misdeeds, deepens our accountability, since we handle only what is His.' Kidner compares this with Daniel 5.23: 'The God in whose hand is your breath . . . you have not honoured'.[24] But, 'because the psalmist envisages the world in the light of God's affirmation of it, he does not stop at the tragic aspect of dying, but discerns in the coming into being and passing away of living things the conquest of death by means of the continual process of re-creation by the ever-active, ever-living God.'[25] It is the psalmist's concern for God's glory, and God's joy in his creation (v. 31) which prompts both his own worship ('I will sing to the LORD as long as I live') and his prayer that sinners and the wicked will be no more. 'The

---

24 Derek Kidner, *Psalms 73–150*, 1975; cf. A. Weiser, *The Psalms*, 1959.
25 Weiser, *The Psalms*, p. 670.

CREATION: THE CONTEXT FOR COVENANT

poet longs for the time when God's joy in his creature and the creature's joy in his Maker (v. 34) will unite in perfect harmony, but he does so not from hatred of the sinners but because of the purity of his joy in God and in his creation.'[26]

Creation as God's covenanted gift

All three perspectives on humanity's role within the created order – of harmony and interdependence, of awesome distance, of 'having dominion' – depend on a picture of creation as God's gift. It is God who plants the garden and puts humanity and the other creatures within it, and charges human beings to serve and to protect it. It is God, as Job is reminded, whose world this is, and human beings are small and dependent creatures within it. It is God the Creator who by his living Word and wisdom, and his life-giving Spirit not only creates all things, but through constantly renewing the face of the earth sustains and preserves all things in being through the constant rhythm of life and death and re-creation.

God places humanity within the created order as his image-bearer to take the responsibility of royal service, royal priesthood, to mediate between God and the rest of creation for God's sake, and to give a voice to creation's praise. Creation, in other words, acts as the context in which God's cosmic covenant is lived out. Creation also becomes the context for the drama of redemption through which God's healing and re-creating love does not abandon a world which has 'fallen' and gone astray, but in which God keeps faith with his people and constantly holds out visions of hope.

God's covenant with his people over time, from Abraham, through Moses and David, into the story of the new covenant in the upper room centred on Jesus Christ who is the image of the invisible God, is the drama of creation being upheld, the face of the earth being renewed, creation itself being redeemed and

---

26 Weiser, *The Psalms*, p. 670.

healed, until God gives a fresh gift of creation in a new heaven and a new earth in which justice dwells, and all things are caught up into the kingdom of his glory.

Covenant is God's way of being faithful to his gift of creation, and inviting us to play our part as his royal servants and priests in working for the coming of his kingdom.

4

Sabbath: covenant joy

> Holy, holy, holy Lord,
> God of power and might,
> Heaven and earth are full of your glory.
> Common Worship, Holy Communion

Life rhythm and lifestyle

Even if we were able to reduce carbon emissions by anything approaching the 90% by 2030 which some advocates are proposing, the earth's temperature would still warm significantly over the next decades because of the damage that industrial carbon emissions have already caused. That will mean inevitable changes to weather conditions and so to food production.

It will mean some changes to sea levels and so more flooding. It is likely to mean increasing migration, both human migration from low-lying lands such as Bangladesh, and also the movement of wild animals as their habitat changes and the desert advances on the savannah. And in the Western world climate change puts to us very urgent questions about our energy supply and, increasingly, energy security. To retain our present dependence on gas in the UK will mean increasing imports of gas from places such as Russia, Ukraine, and the Gulf States. Gas at the moment arrives at Bacton on the Norfolk coast – one of the coastlines most threatened by sea erosion. Our coal-fired power stations have been reduced; our nuclear power stations are coming to the end of their lives; renewable energy resources are not very well developed on a large enough scale; nuclear fusion is many years away.

But behind all this is the deeper question underlined so powerfully by Michael Northcott in *A Moral Climate*. Not only is our dependence on fossil fuels going to prove unsustainable, it is in itself a symptom of a culture and a lifestyle which have lost touch with the rhythms of nature. Much of the Western way of life which has developed since World War II, and which we have all got so used to, has actually contributed to the crisis we are now in. Widespread reliance on oil consumption and the growth of road and air travel, commuting to work, driving to schools and to supermarkets, transporting food across the country from sorting depots to delivery warehouses, moving freight from rail to roads, the rapid growth of overseas holiday flights, and so on, will simply not be sustainable as oil runs out. It is all contributing to growth in carbon emissions and so to global warming. Northcott sees the whole basis of our Western economy, and the rhythm and speed of life in which the consumer culture is now enmeshed, as out of line with the patterns of life which the planet can sustain: 'Industrial consumerism is a form of material culture which is entirely at odds with the regenerative and recycling patterns of natural systems.'[1]

Climate change is therefore putting very large questions to us about our Western lifestyle. Our present rhythms of life are unsustainable. If the present levels of consumption in the UK were copied worldwide, we would need three planet earths to sustain it. Climate change is telling us to change our lifestyles.

Within the covenantal relationship of God with his people, the institution of the Sabbath addresses the question of life's rhythms, and the pattern of life which makes for the best flourishing both of humanity and of the earth. The Sabbath is a way of recognizing that there is more to life than work and consumption; that human health and well-being are linked to the 'health and well-being' and the lifecycles of the earth; that sustenance requires a spiritual as well as a material component. One of the things which Western culture has lost is a sense of the sacred.

---

1 Northcott, *A Moral Climate*, p. 33.

SABBATH: COVENANT JOY

Loss of the sacred

Some people are reacting to the destructiveness of the materialist consumer culture by trying to recover a sense of the sacred through pantheism. There are many people within the environmental movements who do seek some spiritual component in their understanding of the world, but do not wish to invoke the Judaeo-Christian God. 'Pantheism' is the view that everything is God, but that is a view not found in the Bible. The main difficulty with this belief is that if everything is God, then God must include the tsunami and the streptococcus, and there are no categories by which to distinguish the good from the bad. By contrast, the biblical view of creation is that there is an abnormality and ambiguity to this 'fallen world' which needs healing and redeeming, a world which though made by God is not God and is not to be identified with God. Within pantheism, everything in 'nature' becomes evened out into what some people have called 'a polite form of atheism', because God is identified with everything. If God is the same as nature, time tends to become an illusion, because the eternal God becomes the same as a time-limited world. Our human freedom also tends to become an illusion, as the all-knowing and all powerful God is identified with everything that happens, which leads to a sort of fatalism. Also, identifying God with the material world tends to diminish the reality of the spiritual world. Pantheism is not compatible with a biblically based Christianity.

On the other hand, it is vitally important to say that there is something sacred about God's creation. *Creation is not divine, but it is sacred.* It is not God, but in its sacredness can be seen what some people have called a 'sacrament' of God. As was said of Georgia O'Keeffe's paintings of the high desert north of Santa Fe, she depicts the desert as 'holy'.

There is a rich strand of Christian thinking, recently revived in some of the writings about Celtic spirituality,[2] which celebrates the whole of life as the gift of God, and discerns the Spirit

---

2 E.g. Philip Newell, *Listening for the Heartbeat of God*, 1997.

of God, the Lord, the giver of life, in and through all things. Jürgen Moltmann's Gifford Lectures *God in Creation* shows God the Holy Trinity constantly breathing the life of the Spirit into the creation. Everything exists within the life of the cosmic Spirit of God. The Creator Spirit 'interpenetrates, quickens and animates the world', a theological view that was 'pushed out', says Moltmann, by the modern mechanistic world picture.[3] Moltmann describes his view as a form of *panentheism* – God, having created the world also dwells in it – though elsewhere he is critical of a theology which identifies the world with the inner life of God.[4] We need to be able to say both that God is different from and separate from what God has created, and also to say that it is in God that we and all things 'live and move and have our being' (Acts 17.28). As the psalmist says, it is God's Spirit that is sent forth in the creation of all things; it is through the Spirit that God renews the face of the earth (Ps. 104.30).

As Moltmann rightly says, a Trinitarian doctrine of creation in the Spirit and of the Creator Spirit who indwells creation, 'views creation as a dynamic web of interconnected processes'. 'The Spirit differentiates and binds together. The Spirit preserves and leads living things and their communities beyond themselves. This indwelling Creator Spirit is fundamental for the community of creation... If the cosmic Spirit is the Spirit of God, the universe cannot be viewed as a closed system. It has to be understood as a system that is open – open for God and for his future.'[5] Calvin put it this way:

> It is the Spirit who, everywhere diffused, sustains all things, causes them to grow, and quickens them in heaven and in earth. Because he is circumscribed by no limits, he is excepted from the category of creatures; but in transfusing into all things his energy, and breathing into them essence, life and movement, he is... plainly divine.[6]

---

3 Moltmann, *God in Creation*, p. 98.
4 J. Moltmann, *The Trinity and the Kingdom of God*, 1981, p. 107.
5 Moltmann, *God in Creation*, p. 103.
6 J. Calvin, *Institutes of the Christian Religion*, I.13.14.

It is God's Spirit which makes nature sacred. It is God's Spirit which enables us to see creation as holy. James Nash discusses the sacramental nature of the universe by which he means that the whole of material existence is holy because it can become a vehicle of communion with God, a means of grace. He puts it this way:

> This understanding of sacramentality emphatically denies that the Christian faith descralises nature . . . Nature is sacred by association, as the bearer of the sacred. We are standing perpetually on holy ground, because God is present not only in the burning bush but in the nurturing soil and atmosphere, indeed, sharing the joys and agonies of all creatures. The sacramental presence of the Spirit endows all of creation with a sacred value and dignity.[7]

This is an integrated, relational view of the world. The loss of a sense of nature's mystery and sacredness, a loss of the holy, can be traced back in some respects to the growth of modern science and technology, with its associated view of the natural order as a mechanism rather than an organism. Max Weber wrote of 'the disenchantment of nature'. One of the effects of modern Western civilization has been 'to rob nature of any mystic or sacral qualities and to represent it as a resource rightfully at the disposal of humanity'.[8]

One of the theological words which holds onto the sense of the sacred is Sabbath. Michael Northcott comments that

> The practice of Sabbath celebrated the spiritual relation of the world to God by sanctifying time, and the work of the agrarian year. It trained the Israelites to remember that the land was gift and not property, for 'the earth is the Lord's and all that is in it' (Psalm 24.1). In this way the Sabbath laws sanctified time and space, and indicated that work and

---

7 James A. Nash, *Loving Nature*, 1991, p. 115.
8 Alister McGrath, *The Re-enchantment of Nature*, 2002, p. 101.

making are moral as well as material activities, governed by transcendent principles as well as by biological laws and relationships. And when the Hebrews neglected sacred time, their work and making in material space came into conflict with these principles, laws and relationships.[9]

Sabbath

Sabbath, of course, is the name given to the seventh day of the week in which – in the first Genesis narrative of creation – God ceased from his work and declared the day to be holy. 'So God blessed the seventh day and hallowed it' (Gen. 2.3). The seventh day of the week then came to be set apart for God, a joyful day, a holy day, a day for spiritual renewal and for worship.

One of the themes which links creation to covenant, as this is worked out in the life of the covenant people of God, is the Sabbath. If we look at the different reasons given for 'remembering the Sabbath day to keep it holy' in the two versions of the Ten Commandments in the Old Testament, for example, we find one refers to God's creation of the world, and the other refers to God's covenant of redemption. So in Exodus 20 we read, 'Remember the Sabbath day and keep it holy . . . for in six days the Lord made heaven and earth, but rested the seventh day.' Whereas in Deuteronomy 5.12 the context and focus is more covenantal: 'Observe the Sabbath day and keep it holy . . . remember that you were a slave in the land of Egypt, and the LORD your God brought you out from there . . . therefore the LORD your God commanded you to keep the Sabbath day holy.' From the understanding of the meaning of the Sabbath, we see, once again, that the Creator God who made heaven and earth is the covenant God who rescued his people from slavery in Egypt.

God's people, created and redeemed, are to keep the Sabbath day holy. Why? Because the Sabbath stands for various aspects

---

9 Northcott, *A Moral Climate*, p. 11.

of the life of God's people which are essential if God's covenant people are to live in the way their Creator intended for them, for their health and well-being, for the sustainability and health of their environment, and for his glory. It seems that the Sabbath was an institution which particularly marked out the people of God. The covenant purposes of God for his people are rooted in the creative purposes of God for his world. God's creative purpose and God's covenanted love belong together.

Joy

One of the features of Sabbath was the provision of a day for rest and restoration which included joyful corporate worship and celebration. 'For six days shall work be done; but the seventh day is a Sabbath of complete rest, a holy convocation' (Lev. 23.3). By the time Isaiah 58.13 was written, the Sabbath is called 'a delight'. Clearly, 'Sabbath' came to be associated with a festival of the people, celebrating God their creator (Isa. 58.14 goes on to refer to 'delight in the Lord'), and also as a 'sign of the everlasting covenant' made by God with his people (Exod. 31.12–17; cf. Ezek. 20.12). The restorative power of joyful worship was (remarkably) linked to belief that God needed refreshment after the work of creating the world. Exodus 31.17, in an unexpected phrase, says that God paused on the seventh day 'and was refreshed'.

The whole of Genesis 1 leads up to the Sabbath. The writer is saying that the rhythm of six days plus one is the way things are in the world. Human lives are built to reflect that reality. A human being's alternation between work and rest, engagement and restoration, is meant to echo the way God is, and the alternation between work and rest in the creative activity of God. And what is God's rest? It is delight in his creation. It is looking with joy on his world and saying 'This is good'! It is the note struck by the writer in Proverbs, speaking of the divine Wisdom:

> When [the Lord] established the heavens I was there, when he drew a circle on the face of the deep, when he made firm the skies above, when he established the fountains of the deep, when he assigned to the sea its limit, so that the waters might not transgress his command, when he marked out the foundations of the earth, then I was beside him like a master worker, I was daily his delight, rejoicing before him always, rejoicing in his inhabited world and delighting in the human race. (Prov. 8.27–31)

David Hubbard comments verse 31, 'Like a gleeful little kid, wisdom is so excited by the majesty and power of the creation that she jokes and laughs about it daily with the Creator, who takes exquisite delight in her jollity.'[10]

The sense of joyful worship in celebration of the Creator, of which the Sabbath is a reminder, is wonderfully expressed in Job 38.7, where we read that when God formed the earth, 'the morning stars sang together and all the sons of God shouted for joy'.

Worship

Our Sabbath rest is the God-given opportunity which the Creator gives us to share his delight. Human life is meant to include more than labour, more than struggle. It is a rhythm of engagement with the world in work and then thankful enjoyment of the world in worship – offering back to God for him to enjoy our enjoyment of the world. The climax of the Genesis creation narrative is humanity the worshipper: *Homo Adorans*, the one who in fellowship with the Creator enjoys the Creator's work, and can give a voice to the silent order of the universe so that it too, with us, may sing God's praise.

The note of delight in the world, a sense of creation's 'enchantment', has too often been crushed by an approach to

---

10 David Hubbard, *The Communicator's Commentary: Proverbs*, 1989.

the world which sees it either as simply a mechanism to be manipulated, or as a source of fuel and food for human well-being. The people who accuse science of having robbed creation of its wonder believe science has also taken away our joy.

One of the writers who says a great deal about the enjoyment of the world is the seventeenth-century English poet Thomas Traherne:

> You never enjoy the world aright, till the Sea itself floweth in your veins, till you are clothed with the heavens, and crowned with the stars: and perceive yourself to be the sole heir of the whole world, and more than so, because men are in it who are every one sole heirs as well as you. Till you can sing and rejoice and delight in God, as misers do in gold and Kings in sceptres, you never enjoy the world.[11]

Later, Traherne also emphasizes human engagement with and dependence on the rest of the natural order:

> By an Act of the understanding therefore be present now with all the creatures among which you live; and hear them in their beings and operations praising God in an heavenly manner. Some of them vocally, others in their ministry, all of them naturally and continually. We infinitely wrong ourselves by laziness and confinement. All creatures in all nations, and tongues and people praise God infinitely; and the more, for being your sole and perfect treasures. You are never what you ought till you go out of yourself and walk among them.[12]

What are we created for? That we may be creatures of the seventh day! That we may share God's work of bringing order in his creation; that we may grow in personal communion with

---

[11] Thomas Trahene, *Centuries of Meditations*: *The First Century*, p. 29.

[12] Thomas Trahene, *Centuries of Meditations*: *The Second Century*, p. 76.

him and so reflect his image; and that we may share the delight of his rest. That we may have fellowship with the Creator. That we may be caught up in praise with the sun and moon and stars, the trees and flowers and birds; with all creatures great and small, fish and beasts. All these look to God for their life and sustenance; all these in their silent ways sing the song of their Creator.

Enough is enough

The Sabbath points us also to the importance of sufficiency and contentment. As long ago as 1975, John Taylor wrote *Enough is Enough*,[13] in which he explored the sins of excess, especially in cultures where consumption of food and accumulation of goods become the highest values, and in which waste and pollution, our plundering of the planet's natural resources of fuels and minerals, and our expenditure on the arms trade is all leading to 'ruthless, unbridled, unthinking excess'. 'We are being made to expect too much. We are taking too much. We are scrapping too much. We are paying and compelling others to pay far too high a price.'

He reminds us of the way that many of the laws which are collected together in the book of Deuteronomy express, rather, a culture of sufficiency and contentment. He is not calling for asceticism nor a deliberate return to poverty, but simply a recognition that we and others need 'enough' – but that 'enough is enough'. In the law of gleaning, for example, the farmer was not to reap to the very edges of his field, but to leave something 'for the alien, the orphan and the widow'. 'That is to say: remember what kind of God I am; remember the world of human and ecological relationships in which you enjoy the covenant with me. Enough is enough, and the less fortunate will be glad of what is left. The reason for this moderation is the memory of their own dependency. They are no self-made men:

---

13 John V. Taylor, *Enough is Enough*, 1975.

SABBATH: COVENANT JOY

they owe everything to God. Remember that you were slaves in Egypt; *that* is why I command you to do this' (Lev. 19.9–10; Deut. 25.19–22).[14]

Then there was the Sabbath of Sabbaths. 'When you enter the land that I am giving you, the land shall observe a Sabbath for the LORD. For six years you shall sow your field and for six years you shall prune your vineyard and gather in their yield; but in the seventh year there shall be a Sabbath of complete rest for the land, a Sabbath for the LORD: you shall not sow your field or prune your vineyard. You shall not reap the aftergrowth of your harvest or gather the grapes of your unpruned vine: it shall be a year of complete rest for the land. You may eat what the land yields during its Sabbath – you, your male and female slaves, your hired and your bound labourers who live with you; for your livestock also, and for the wild animals in your land all its yield shall be for food' (Lev. 25.1–7).

It is interesting how the Sabbath command is now applied to the land, and incorporated within it is a motive of care for the poor. This was expressed in Exodus 23.12 in these terms: 'For six days you shall do your work, but on the seventh day you shall rest, so that your ox and your donkey may have relief, and your home-born slave and the resident alien may be refreshed.' This altruistic motive is picked up also in Deuteronomy's version of the Ten Commandments (Deut. 5.12ff.). As von Rad pointed out in his commentary, the version of the Ten Commandments in Exodus 20 is 'thoroughly theological' – rooting the Sabbath in the nature of God – but the Deuteronomic version is more 'psychological', bringing out the benefits of Sabbath rest for human and animal life.[15]

The Church of England Report *Sharing God's Planet* put it this way:

Humankind is easily ensnared in the culture of ownership. Even if it is understood intellectually that the world is God's

---

14 Taylor, *Enough is Enough*, p. 50.
15 G. von Rad, *Deuteronomy*, 1966, p. 58.

and the human role of stewardship means to have dominion only under him, people can still find themselves caught by desire [for possessions], which is by its nature voracious . . . In the midst of this, the Christian is called to stop: completely, properly, for a period of time. Not just to pause for breath before carrying on consuming, but to take a deep dive into God's peace.[16]

Jubilee

One further dimension to the concept of Sabbath is seen in the law relating to Jubilee, which leads into some issues of political economy which I will pick up further in the next chapter. The law about Jubilee proclaimed liberty to the people who had become enslaved through debt, and it restored land to families who had been obliged to sell it out of necessity in the previous 50 years.

The law is spelled out in Leviticus 25.8–55. The people were to count seven weeks of years, that is 49 years. Then the trumpet (*yobel*) was to be sounded on the tenth day of the seventh month, the Day of Atonement. The fiftieth year was to be made 'holy'. 'And you shall proclaim release [liberty] through all the land. It shall be a jubilee for you . . . you shall return to your property . . . and to your family.' In the jubilee the people were not to sow, or reap aftergrowth, or harvest unpruned vines. They were to return to their ancestral homes. The land was not to be sold in perpetuity, 'for the land is mine' (v. 23), 'with me you are but tenants and sojourners'.

If one of the people was reduced to poverty and sold part of his property but could not afford to redeem it, it was to remain in the hands of the purchaser until the year of jubilee when it would revert to the original owner (v. 28).

If a kinsman falls into difficulty and becomes dependent, 'you shall support them' (v. 35), but if they are so impoverished that

---

16 *Sharing God's Planet*, p. 27.

they sell themselves, 'you shall not make them serve as slaves. They shall remain with you as hired or bound labourers. They shall serve with you until the year of jubilee. Then they and their children with them shall be free from your authority; they shall go back to their own family. For they are my servants, whom I brought out of the land of Egypt' (v. 39f.).

There has been considerable discussion about the origin of this law, and whether or not it was ever enacted. Whatever the answers to these questions, it stands in the text as a symbol and sign of various Sabbath principles of which we do well to take note. The law depicts Jubilee as essentially an economic institution for the sake of the family and of the land.

As Patrick Logan argues,[17] in the book of Leviticus, the trumpet call to Jubilee was first of all a call to repentance – the *yobel* is the horn that is sounded on the Day of Atonement (Lev. 23.27). And radical repentance is seen in the principles of release. There is release for the ground, that is given a year of recovery from farming. There is release from the build up of capital only in the hands of the few, and every jubilee it reverts to its original owner, because ultimately the land belongs to the Lord. There is the release of hired labourers from their servitude, because they, too, belong to the Lord.

Logan maintains that Jubilee was clearly the restoration of community to a divided people.[18] It required the overcoming of both the spiritual and material causes of alienation. It was not a call to the powerless to rise up; rather, a call for the powerful to let go. Its core aims were the rehabilitation of family ties. It dealt with the roots of poverty, not just its manifestations. It dealt with not only personal, but structural sin.

The implications of Jubilee thinking for political economy are clear, if we remember that political economy means focusing on power. 'Economies and markets are never morally or politically neutral. They are . . . woven into a society's system of

---

17 Patrick Logan, *Biblical Reflections on the Political Economy of Jubilee*, 1997.
18 Logan, *Biblical Reflections*, pp. 2f.

relationships, beliefs and power. Until we realise how they are constructed socially, culturally and politically, we will be locked into a helpless and irresponsible dependency on forces that are passively accepted as beyond question or control.'[19]

Jubilee in Israel addressed questions of economic inequality and the injustices which derived from concentrations of political and economic power by requiring repentance, release, and the recognition that both land and people belonged to God. 'Practices of release, in the case of Israel as well as her neighbours, provided important mechanisms for promoting social, economic and political stability (or as we might say today "cohesion"). On the one hand, they prevented debtors from becoming too weak; on the other hand, they prevented creditors from becoming too strong.'[20]

Clearly in Israel, the land was central in political economy. Today we might refer to energy, oil or water as a central factor.

Jubilee thus relates the Sabbath principles to justice for people (which I will discuss further in Chapter 5) in a practical concern for families, and to conservation of the land.

Michael Northcott's argument that Western civilization and way of life are based on a belief in unrestricted economic growth, such that the richer world gets richer at the expense of the poorer parts of the world which become even poorer, illustrates the contemporary significance of Jubilee.

Jesus' Sabbath ministry

The way Jesus uses the Sabbath and the Jubilee principles in his ministry is instructive. It was 'his custom' (Luke 4.16) to worship in the synagogue on the Sabbath day, where he often taught (Mark 1.21). But it was also particularly noted by the Gospel writers that it was on a Sabbath day that, when his disciples were hungry, as they went through the cornfields, Jesus plucked the heads of grain to eat, coming into conflict with the Pharisees

---

19 Logan, *Biblical Reflections*, p. 3.
20 Logan, *Biblical Reflections*, p. 11.

who argued that was unlawful (Matt. 12.1f.). Matthew then records Jesus healing a man with a withered hand in the synagogue on the Sabbath day (Matt. 12.9f.), leading to his reply to the Pharisees' accusation: 'It is lawful to do good on the Sabbath' (Matt. 12.12). The fourth Gospel tells of Jesus healing a blind man on the Sabbath (John 9.14). Mark's Gospel records Jesus as saying, 'The Sabbath was made for humankind, and not humankind for the Sabbath' (Mark 2.27). In other words, Jesus, the 'Lord of the Sabbath' (Matt. 12.8), uses Sabbath time for nourishment and for healing. He feeds his disciples and he restores and renews the lives of those who are ill. Sabbath, then, for Jesus, includes restoration, renewal, nourishment and health-giving.

It is no accident that it was on the Sabbath day that Luke's Gospel describes Jesus going to the synagogue in Capernaum, and applies a reading from Isaiah 61 to his own ministry. He describes himself as both fulfilling Isaiah's prophecy of God's coming kingly priest (a passage in Isaiah which illustrates the prophetic use of the Jubilee principles), and also as fulfilling something of the Jubilee provision as well:

> The Spirit of the Lord is upon me, because he has anointed me to bring good news to the poor. He has sent me to proclaim release to the captives and recovery of sight to the blind, to let the oppressed go free, to proclaim the year of the Lord's favour . . . Today this scripture has been fulfilled in your hearing. (Luke 4.14–21)

The reference to 'freedom' picks up the Jubilee concept. It is not likely that Jesus was calling on the whole of Israel to observe a Jubilee year. It is more possible that he was expecting his followers to live by the Jubilee principle among themselves,[21] and saying that his own ministry would be one which leads to a generosity of sharing, a release from debts, a forgiveness of sins. John Howard Yoder even concludes that Jesus is

---

21 N.T. Wright, *Jesus and the Victory of God*, 1996, pp. 294f.

introducing a new regime for his followers, 'whose marks would be that rich would give to the poor, the captives would be freed, and men would have a new mentality (*metanoia*), if they believed this news.'[22] Certainly we read of the early Christians in the Acts of the Apostles developing a lifestyle of generosity:

> All who believed were together and had all things in common; they would sell their possessions and goods and distribute the proceeds to all, as any had need. Day by day as they spent much time together in the temple, they broke bread at home and ate their food with glad and generous hearts, praising God and having the goodwill of all the people. (Acts 2.44f.)

It is also important, as Yoder argues, that 'as in the Jubilee and as in the Lord's Prayer, *debt* is seen as the paradigmatic social evil'.[23] He is referring to the translation of the Lord's Prayer which prays 'Your kingdom come. Your will be done, on earth as it is in heaven. Give us this day our daily bread. And forgive us our debts, as we also have forgiven our debtors' (Matt. 6.10f.). Judaism knew 'sin' in terms of 'debt to God', but it is possible that the Lord's Prayer reaches more widely than personal sins, into the Jubilee concepts of release and liberation from debt. At the very least, for Christians to pray for daily bread and for forgiveness commits us to generosity of heart and concern for and fellowship with our neighbours, especially the poor and oppressed of God's world. Climate change is reminding us increasingly forcefully who and where such neighbours are. It is facing us with the 'carbon debt' owed by the industrialized West to the rest of the world.

---

22 John Howard Yoder, *The Politics of Jesus*, 1972, p. 39.
23 Yoder, *The Politics of Jesus*, p. 41.

Nourishment and health

We saw that 'Sabbath' for Jesus included concerns for both nourishment and health. Two of the major features of damaging climate change will be

- the effects on agriculture and food production
- the spread of disease.

Food

John Houghton describes the impacts of climate change on agriculture and food supply, along with economic and other factors, in terms of the need to match crops to new climatic conditions, though trees and forests may find themselves in a climate to which they are far from suited, as of course trees and forests take much longer to adapt than crops which mature in a matter of months or years. He refers to the way Peruvian farmers have had to adapt their cotton or rice production according to the cycle of El Niño events.

The factors which will most affect food production are the availability of water, possibly the boost to some crops by increased atmospheric carbon dioxide, but the huge reduction in yields due to increased temperatures for others. Flooding would be a very significant factor in many parts of the world. A rise in sea level could flood much of Bangladesh's best agricultural land. In some places the salt concentration of the waters in coastal regions means that where once rice was harvested, now the main harvest is shrimps. The *Guardian*[24] carried a headline 'Droughts, floods, soaring crop prices and the rising demand for biofuels combine to make life harder for the poor and threaten political instability'. The article included this paragraph: 'Empty shelves in Varacas. Food riots in West Bengal and Mexico. Warnings of hunger in Jamaica, Nepal, the Philippines and sub-Saharan Africa. Soaring prices for basic foods are

---
24 *The Guardian Weekly*, 9.11.07.

beginning to lead to political instability, with governments being forced to step in to control artificially the cost of bread, maize, rice and dairy products.' One of the factors leading to rising world grain prices is the seventh year (in 2007) of drought in Australia, devastating the wheat crop. Southern Australia has lost one-fifth of its rainfall in recent decades. 'Drought is the new climate,' said environmentalist Tim Flannery. Our prayer for daily bread, and our Lord's concern that his disciples should not go hungry, must lead us urgently to fresh ways of thinking through how all God's people are to be fed.

Health

Climate change is also already having an impact on health. The record temperatures in Europe in 2003 were blamed for 21,000 additional deaths due to the heat. On the other hand, some mortality due to severe cold might be reduced, though warmer winters may help micro-organisms to flourish in ways adverse to human health. 'The likelihood of extremes of climate, such as droughts and floods, will also bring greater risks to health from increased malnutrition and from a prevalence of conditions more likely to lead to the spread of diseases from a variety of causes.'[25] Many insect carriers thrive better in warmer temperatures, and tropical diseases, such as malaria and yellow fever, could more easily spread to higher latitudes. In January 2007 it was reported that malaria, which had been eradicated from Italy in 1970, was making a comeback. There was also an increase in tick-borne encephalitis and visceral leishmaniasis, carried by sandflies. 'Climate change brings malaria back to Italy' was the headline in the article, which included the comment that 20% of the fish now swimming in the Mediterranean, including barracuda, are types that have migrated from the Red Sea as water temperatures rise. Malaria has also returned to Peru,[26] from which it was eradicated 40 years ago. In 2007,

---

25 Houghton, *Global Warming*, p. 176.
26 *The Guardian Weekly*, 9.11.07.

64,000 cases were recorded, blamed on constant climate change, and on deforestation which forces the mosquitoes to move to new areas. Al Gore's *An Inconvenient Truth* suggests that some 30 so-called 'new diseases' have emerged over the last 25 to 30 years, and gives an example of the West Nile virus which entered the United States in Maryland on the east coast in 1999, and within four years had spread to the Pacific Coast.[27] If climate change is having an impact on health, it will also significantly impact healthcare delivery and put pressure on health services. If the coming Kingdom of God, for which we are taught to pray and look, includes the healing of the nations (Rev. 22.2), that commits us to follow Jesus' example of compassion for and healing of the sick. Some of the signs of the Kingdom are that 'the blind receive their sight, the lame walk, the lepers are cleansed, the deaf hear, the dead are raised, and the poor have good news brought to them' (Matt. 11.5f.). The covenant of creation is upheld, and God's healing brought to people and nations – and to the whole created order – as God's Kingdom comes 'on earth as it is in heaven'.

A technological mind-set

The Sabbath provision holds out before us a constant reminder that the earth is the Lord's, that there is more to life than material consumption, that we need to recover our sense of the sacred, the holy, so that our lives can more fully be in tune with the rhythms of the earth, and that the rich resources of God's earth are to be shared.

One of the further questions which climate change is bringing into sharp focus is our growing trust in technology to solve our problems. I do not want to be misunderstood. I thank God for the work of science, and for the technologies which have contributed so much to human well-being, in medicine, transport, communication, and so on. However, as we discovered when

---

27 Al Gore, *An Inconvenient Truth*, 2006.

chlorofluorocarbons were being released from domestic refrigerators into the atmosphere in large quantities, and had such a destructive effect on the ozone layer, sometimes technology can have very negative effects as well as positive.

The nuclear fission which creates energy can also be used for weapons of mass destruction. While the world's first wave-farm is created in the sea off Portugal, environmentalists express severe concern about the devastation to local wildlife should the proposed barrage across Britain's River Severn be constructed.[28] Technology can be a marvellous servant, but becomes a destructive master. What can become most destructive of all is the 'technological mind-set', which tends to see everything in terms of technology and technique. There is a way of thinking, stemming initially from the Enlightenment view of the world as a large mechanism, which sees humanity's role in relation to the rest of the created order in terms of technological manipulation. What get lost are the human values of community, fellowship, and a recognition of the sacred. We begin to see what is not us in terms of what we can do with it. Science as a quest for truth is now frequently getting swallowed up by technology. 'What is truth?' is taken over by 'What is useful?' Research money is provided for projects which fit in with certain political ideologies. 'Technique' and 'skill' become more important than understanding or wisdom. And then what becomes of science?

It was 30 years ago that the research chemist Walter Thorson wrote:

> Having finally understood that scientific truth is a source of power, man has made the crucial decision that from now on the will to power and the uses of power should dictate the relevance and value of that truth. Because of that decision, 'pure' science, the science of the past four hundred years, will begin to be altered in subtle ways, and will eventually disappear.[29]

---

28 *Natural World*, 2007, p. 8.
29 W. Thorson, 'The Spiritual Dimensions of Science', in C.F. Henry (ed.), *Horizons of Science*, 1978, pp. 217f.

SABBATH: COVENANT JOY

If Thorson is right in this, sometimes we are seeing in our science research programmes a cost-benefit manipulation of truth for the sake of practical or political usefulness. 'The fusion of science and technology means that increasingly the moral decision as to the uses of truth will be made pre-emptively before the truth itself is even sought; we shall seek only truth which fits our purposes.'[30]

One interesting contemporary example of 'projects which fit political ideologies' was given in a report in *The New Yorker* on 5 November 2007:

> In 1993 President Clinton launched the Partnership for a New Generation of Vehicles. It was designed to assist the big three automakers in producing cars that would increase fuel efficiency threefold in 10 years. In 2002, after $1 billion of federal money had been spent and each of the Big Three had produced models of fuel-efficient cars, the Bush administration scrapped the program in favour of the FreedomCAR project, which is aimed at creating a car that runs on pure hydrogen. Meanwhile, the average car sold in the US today gets 20 miles per gallon – about the same as in 1993 when Clinton launched the Partnership program, and less than Henry Ford's Model T got when it went on the market 99 years ago.[31]

Here is one example in Western culture where oil profits are given a higher priority than the needs of the planet. Michael Northcott wrote about the 'gods of secular reason, technological power and monetary accumulation' which, he argued, tend to sideline traditional understandings of community, justice and the sacred.[32] He also warns against the 'technical fixes' which are widely regarded as the solutions to global warming. Some people think that hydrogen cells are the answer for cars, but of course energy will be needed for the production of hydro-

---

30 Thorson, 'The Spiritual Dimensions', pp. 217f.
31 Reported in *Christian Century*, 27 November 2007.
32 Northcott, *A Moral Climate*, p. 14.

gen, and there are huge questions about its storage and distribution. The use of biofuels may give us more energy-efficiency, but face us with the problems of weighing the priorities in land use for their production over the production of food. In some places people go hungry because biofuels are being grown on land previously used for food crops. Carbon sequestration (capturing carbon from emissions from power stations and storing it underground) may be possible, and if so would be a very sensible contribution, but its long-term safety is unknown. The 'holy grail' of nuclear fusion – controlling the power released by fusion of hydrogen atoms, which the 'high-powered laser energy research' teams are working on – is still decades away. Northcott also makes this sober point:

> These proposed engineering solutions to the climate crisis seem to present industrial societies with ways of resolving global warming while avoiding radical changes to the industrial way of life . . . They would allow the politics of speed to continue to subvert the politics of place, and the health of other species and ecosystems. They sustain the illusion that modern humans in their quest for technological efficiency do not have the time to tend to the objective and contingent needs of the planet and its creatures. And they maintain the illusion that humanity is in control of the planet . . . and that there are no biological or climatological limits to the aspirations of industrial humans for speed and wealth.[33]

We need more than technology to solve the climate crisis – important though the service of technology will inevitably be. We need a recovery of the sacred, the holy, the realization that everything cannot be simply reduced to materialism and consumption. We need a context of respect for the earth and its creatures and for our neighbours, especially the poor and disadvantaged. We need to recover a sense of God's delight in creation, and learn again to share God's joy. And we need radically to revise our industrial lifestyle.

---

33 Northcott, *A Moral Climate*, p. 276.

5

Justice: allegiance to the covenant Lord

> You shall love the Lord your God with all your heart, with all your soul, with all your mind, and with all your strength. Love your neighbour as yourself. Amen. Lord, have mercy.
>
> Common Worship, Holy Communion

One of the important features of global warming which we need to address within the framework of our covenant theology is that climate change raises questions of justice. It requires us to address the moral implications of the fact that the people most affected by global warming will not live in the rich West, but in sub-Saharan Africa, south-east Asia, South America, and the Canadian Arctic. Those people for whom the damaging effects of climate change are already being felt, and will increasingly be most acutely felt, are those people who are already among the poorest and most disadvantaged of the world. For a long time Christians have been concerned to provide aid and relief to the poorest parts of the world.

For a long time Christians have engaged in policies and practices aimed at assisting the developing world. Christians were prominent among the advocates for the alleviation and cancellation of debt to the World Bank owed by the Heavily Indebted Poor Countries which was inspired by the Jubilee 2000 Campaign. Organisations such as Christian Aid and Tearfund have long been assisting the Church to keep these issues in the forefront of our minds and our mission. But the questions raised by climate change underline all this in a fresh way. People are now rightly talking about 'climate justice'.

The linking together of environmental and developmental issues has been the agenda of the World Council of Churches for many years. In their response to the Third Assessment Report from the Intergovernmental Panel on Climate Change, the World Council of Churches wrote, in January 2002:

> Spiritually, the struggle against environmental degradation, in particular, the impact of climate change, must address the contradictions in society, especially the present economic course e.g. non-sustainable consumption in many countries, the increasing gap between rich and poor, the net flow of money from poor to rich countries. Every effort needs to be made to maintain the quality of solidarity in a world whose quality of life is steadily deteriorating.[1]

That plea is very close to the call made to the people of God by some of the prophets of the Old Testament. The covenant obligation on the people of God in response to the Creator God's redeeming grace and loving faithfulness is frequently described in terms of the call to live justly. Nowhere is this clearer than in the prophets of the eighth century BC. In the southern Kingdom of Judah, the prophet Micah has this sublime summary: 'He has told you, O mortal, what is good; and what does the LORD require of you but to do justice, and to love kindness, and to walk humbly with your God?' (Micah 6.8).

Amos

This theme is filled out more fully and more devastatingly in the oracles of Amos, the prophet of the northern Kingdom of Israel, predicting the coming exile of God's people as a mark of divine judgement.

Amos lived during an interesting time in Israel's history, around 750 BC during the prosperous reign of King Jeroboam II.

---

[1] World Council of Churches, *Solidarity with Victims of Climate Change*, 2002.

JUSTICE

On the eastern border, Syria was having to give up its military pressure on Israel in order to protect itself from Assyria. In the south, Judah was strong and acted as a buffer state against Egypt. Israel was having a time of political security unknown since the Golden Age of King Solomon 200 years before. The military threat of 40 years earlier seemed a very long time away. Trade and commerce were flourishing (Amos 8.5f.). Labour was moving from the land to the cities. There was increasing demand for luxury goods (6.4f.). However, growing self-interest was creating a powerful aristocracy of wealth (6.1f.), and this was leading to the disappearance of what we would call the middle class. There were many things about social life and social institutions which Amos could not support, and he stood out against them. He was not a 'professional prophet' – he was a shepherd and cultivated sycamore trees. He simply said what he felt called by God to say, and did so with courage and passion – though, it has to be said, with little immediate success. I will focus on three areas of particular concern to Amos:

1 *The growing gap between rich and poor, and the powerlessness of poverty*

The social leaders were living in pride and luxury (3.15; 6.4–6). But what troubled Amos was not affluence as such, but the oppression of the poor to which it leads (5.11f.). The houses of the rich were being turned into robbers' dens (3.10). The political leaders were as bad as any (6.1). They celebrated their prosperity with an insulation from the suffering of others on which it had been built (4.1). So Amos delivered a ringing rebuke to the people of Israel.

> Thus says the LORD: For three transgressions of Israel, and for four, I will not revoke the punishment; because they sell the righteous for silver and the needy for a pair of sandals – they who trample the head of the poor into the dust of the earth and push the afflicted out of the way. (2.6ff.)

This is Amos's first concern – the growing gap between the rich and the poor and the consequent powerlessness of the poor, and it makes him angry.

This is a major concern for intergovernmental negotiations in relation to climate change. Amos would urge us to recognize the powerlessness of poverty and the consequent responsibility on the richer nations to seek to alleviate it, and to work for truly fair and sustainable development as well as for justice in adaptation to climate change.

2 The social institutions were promoting injustice

Amos's second area of concern was that the social system was actually preventing aid being given to those who needed it.

The court in the gate was the place of justice where righteous order should be established (5.15). The gate was the centre of city life; the townsfolk gathered there (Ps. 127.5). There the poor would wait for aid (Prov. 22.22), and there justice was administered (Deut. 22.15, 24). It was at the gate that the weakest and the poorest should have their defence and find their right. One acid test of the society's soul was how it administered justice. Justice is for people, and yet Amos has to say that absurd as it may seem – as absurd as a horse running over the rocks, or oxen ploughing the sea – 'you have turned justice into poison, and the fruit of righteousness into wormwood' (6.12f.). The courts at the gate are no longer places where justice is done, and where rights are upheld, but have become instead places where the poor are even further enslaved (5.12).

We need constantly to hold our governmental institutions and transnational corporations accountable for the effects their decisions have on the welfare of the poorest. 'The hallmark of fairness is assisting the most vulnerable because they are in the greatest need.'[2]

---

2 W. Neil Adger, Jouni Paavola, Saleemal Huq and M.J. Mace (eds), *Fairness in Adaptation to Climate Change*, 2006, p. 13.

JUSTICE

3 The religious institutions of Amos's day had become hijacked for political ends

Amos refers to Bethel (5.5f), one of the holy shrines of the covenant community. Yet Bethel had ceased to be the place where the Lord was sought (5.4); instead it had been turned into a shrine for the king (7.13)! The secularization and corruption of even holy places of worship meant that the people were beginning to look to the Lord only for material successes, and to another god, Baal, for the rest. The Lord was being manipulated and kept to just a corner of their concerns. So Amos pleads, 'Seek the LORD and live – do not seek Bethel' (5.4–6).

The Lord will not hear their praise any longer at these corrupt shrines. The picture is of a community which has become immune to the needs of the poor, has turned a blind eye to oppression, and transformed justice into poison and, through the idolization of material prosperity even in the holy places, has cut itself off from the worship of God, and therefore also from God's blessing.

The 'Day of the Lord' to which the people looked with hope will in fact, says Amos, be a day of judgement (5.18ff.).

In many ways, Western culture has become infected by a materialist consumerism which has effectively become a new god, a new idol of our age. Part of the Church's task is to recognize the lure of other gods, and to hear and respond again to Amos's call to 'Seek the LORD and live'. The present-day Church needs to get its own house in order and then pick up the prophetic mantle of calling ourselves and each other to live justly.

I want now to stand back and ask about the theological basis for Amos's concerns. What theological ground is he standing on as he makes his lonely protest? What understanding of God undergirds his brave witness for God in a social context which seems to have abandoned him? Unsurprisingly, we find Amos's God is both the Creator God and the covenant Lord.

The sovereign creator

Amos refers to God as 'God of hosts' – that is, God of all gods. He is the creator of the earth, and his name is the name of the covenant Lord, Yahweh, the LORD.

> For lo, the one who forms the mountains, creates the wind, reveals his thoughts to mortals, makes the morning darkness and treads on the heights of the earth – the LORD, the God of hosts, is his name. (Amos 4.13)

> The one who made the Pleiades and Orion, and turns deep darkness into the morning, and darkens the day into night, who calls for the waters of the sea, and pours them out upon the surface of the earth, the LORD is his name, who makes destruction flash out against the strong. (Amos 5.8)

The sense of divine sovereignty is clear in the way the book of Amos opens, for Amos speaks of the roaring of the Lord, uttering his voice from Jerusalem (1.2), not only to Israel, but first to Damascus, Gaza, Tyre, Edom, Ammon, Moab and Judah (chapters 1–2). These are nations mostly without the special revelation of God's purposes which Israel had enjoyed; they were outside the immediate context of God's covenant purposes for Israel, but they were still accountable to God, still part of his concern, still under his decree. For the God made known in creation and in covenant to Israel is the LORD of *all*, all people and all creatures – indeed, the purpose of the covenant with Israel and God's gift of land (as God had said to Abraham) was that through them *all* peoples would be blessed.

God's holy and just nature stand behind Amos's call for righteousness and justice

Amos reminds Israel of their covenant relationship, and therefore covenant obligation.

JUSTICE

> Hear this word that the LORD has spoken against you, O people of Israel, against the whole family that I brought up out of the land of Egypt: 'You only have I known of all the families of the earth, therefore I will punish you for all your iniquities.' (Amos 3.1)

Here is the covenant Lord reminding the covenant people of the intimacy of their relationship with God on the basis of which God's judgement against sin is to be announced. Behind Amos's call for justice is his knowledge of God as rescuer from Egypt and as covenant maker. Justice is not a philosophical concept, but expresses the Creator's faithfulness to the creation, and God's covenanted faithfulness to his people. The covenant relationship, established with Abraham and filled out at the time of the Exodus, linked a promise with a command: 'I will be your God, you will be my people'; 'Be holy as I the Lord your God am holy.'

The God who redeemed his people from slavery in Egypt takes them to Mount Sinai and within the covenant relationship gives them the *torah* – the fatherly instruction for covenant people which indicates the pattern of life which reflects God's character. The call to holiness is to reflect the holiness of God; the call to justice is to reflect the justice of God. This is clearly seen in the so-called Holiness Code of Leviticus 19, in which all the various areas of life are brought under the refrain 'I am the LORD'. Because the Lord is as he is, you should live like this. A covenant ethic is not an ethic of obedience to a detached law code; it is a personal ethic of allegiance to a personal God.

And this is where Amos targets his rebuke: the gracious redeeming God, who has known you and cared for you, is a just and righteous God, so you must live justly and righteously: 'Let justice roll down like waters and righteousness like an ever-flowing stream' (5.24).

More than that: to live in the light of God's character makes for the best for human flourishing. Amos here is in line with Deuteronomy, where the writer says:

> The LORD your God is God of gods and Lord of lords, the great, the mighty and the terrible God who is not partial and takes no bribe. He executes justice for the fatherless and the widow, and loves the sojourner, giving him food and clothing. Love the sojourner, therefore, for you were sojourners in the land of Egypt. (Deut. 10.17)

And again, 'You shall walk in all the ways which the LORD your God has commanded you, that it may go well with you' (Deut. 5.33).

Karl Barth has given this point classic expression:

> The human righteousness required by God and established in obedience, the righteousness which according to Amos 5.24 should pour down as a mighty stream – has necessarily the character of vindication of right in favour of the threatened innocent, the oppressed poor, widows, orphans and aliens. For this reason, in the relations and events in the life of his people, God always takes his stand unconditionally and passionately on this side and on this side alone: against the lofty and on behalf of the lowly; against those who already enjoy right and privilege and on behalf of those who are denied and deprived of it.[3]

The preciousness of humanity

Amos's third theological assumption is that there is a shared common humanity to which he can appeal, and that all creation is precious to God (esp. chapters 2–3). As he surveys Damascus and Gaza, Amos says in effect, 'You know that people matter more than things.' As he looks to Edom and Ammon, he says, 'You know that hatred and cruelty and oppression are evil.' To Moab he says, 'You know that institutionalized bitterness will only be destructive.'

---

3 Barth, *Church Dogmatics* II/1, p. 386.

JUSTICE

Amos's denunciation of the atrocities or war-crimes committed by these other nations (in Amos chapters 2–3) is 'regarded as a matter of human moral consensus . . . None of the offences committed is mentioned in the Old Testament law . . . The logic of the prophet's attack seems to be that all these nations knew or ought to have known that certain practices in time of war, such as enslaving whole populations or torturing conquered enemies, are unacceptable.'[4] Amos is assuming that the nations have a moral conscience to which appeal can be made. Here are hints towards what later Christian tradition would call 'natural law'. There are sins and crimes against humanity. When at the end of his prophecies, Amos opens a glimmer of hope, hope of a restoration which God will give, what is restored are human relationships, renewed cities which can be inhabited again by people, wine and fruit to gladden human hearts. The preciousness of the earth is implicit in Amos's linking of God's blessing of people to his blessing of the land in fertility and fruitfulness:

> I will restore the fortunes of my people Israel, and they shall rebuild the ruined cities and inhabit them; they shall plant vineyards and drink their wine, and they shall make gardens and eat their fruit. I will plant them upon their land, and they shall never again be plucked up out of the land that I have given them, say the LORD your God. (Amos 9.14f.)

Justice is the social expression of love

The word Amos uses which is translated as 'justice' includes much more than 'fairness' – it refers to the righteous character of God translated into the structures of human societies and the behaviour of human beings. God's justice is not static, but dynamic, transformative, redemptive. It is, as F. R. Barry put it, 'the social and political expression of love'. So much of Amos's call for justice is subsumed under Jesus' summary of the *torah* covenant requirement, quoting both Deuteronomy and Leviticus:

---

4 Cf. John Barton, *Ethics and the Old Testament*, 1998, pp. 61f.

'You shall love the Lord your God with all your heart, and with all your soul, and with all your mind'. This is the greatest and first commandment. And a second is like it; 'You shall love your neighbour as yourself'. On these two commandments hang all the law and the prophets. (Matthew 22.37f.)

Jesus' own ministry exemplifies in numerous ways God's inclusive love for all. Jesus breaks the rules and taboos by touching the lepers, by conversing with a woman – a Samaritan at that – and by reaching out to the dead body of the son of the widow of Nain, by eating and drinking with despised tax-collectors and prostitutes. He is at home with the outcasts and those on edges of society. His own ministry was described as 'love, to the end' (John 13.1), and his death a demonstration that 'No one has greater love than this, to lay down one's life for one's friends' (John 15.13). It was God's love for the world (the cosmos, and the whole of human society) that sent his son into the world (John 3.16). Love, says St Paul, is the fulfilling of the law (Rom. 13.10).

God's justice thus transforms our human justice, motivating us to move nearer to his justice in our human society, drawing us to firmer allegiance to the covenant Lord. God's justice is more than civic fairness; it is the basis for *shalom*. God's justice is redemptive ('A just God and a Saviour', Isa. 45.21). As with love, we are only ever 'on the way'. Yet Amos holds out the hope of a day when all will be restored and renewed.

Amos had little political success. Samaria, the capital, was soon to fall to invaders, and the kingdom of Israel was dismantled. But he stood in the breach at a crucial time and bore witness to God's justice and righteousness.

Implications of the covenant calling to live justly

We need now to draw out some of the implications of the prophetic calling to live justly in relation to the questions posed for us by climate change. The main themes I wish to concentrate

JUSTICE

on are first, sustainable development; secondly, action to mitigate climate change (that is, how to act justly in the decisions taken to reduce greenhouse gas emissions); and, thirdly, what is needed to adapt to climate change (that is, how to act justly as we all have to adjust to changes in climate which are inevitable, and make decisions how we live and act in the light of them). We will then take note of three other relevant issues: population, deforestation, and economic reform. What does allegiance to the Lord mean in this context?

Sustainable development

Shalom

There is a biblical vision for a just and sustainable society: it is the peace of the Messiah's kingdom, shaped by the concept '*shalom*'. This Hebrew word describes God's kingdom established and upheld 'with justice and with righteousness' (Isa. 9.7). *Shalom*, often translated 'peace', covers much more than merely the absence of conflict. *Shalom* is rather the absence of disorder at all levels of life and relationship. Positively, *shalom* includes everything God gives for human well-being, and for the health and sustainability of the environment, in all areas of life. It means well-being in the fullest and widest sense of the word. When the Lord brings peace, there is prosperity (Ps. 72.1–7), there is health (Isa. 57.19), there is conciliation (Gen. 26.29), there is contentedness (Gen. 15.15; Ps. 4.8). When the *shalom* of the Lord is present, there are good relationships between nations and people (1 Chron. 12.17–18). God's *shalom* has a personal, a social and an environmental context. 'Seek the *shalom* of the city where I have sent you into exile', writes Jeremiah, 'and pray to the LORD on its behalf, for in its welfare you will find your welfare' (Jer. 29.7).

Peace, then, is about being in right relationships – within oneself, with one's neighbours, with one's environment, with God. Under God, social sustainability and environmental sustainability belong together. Peace at its highest is about the enjoyment and satisfaction of being in right relationships. True peace is inseparably linked to righteousness: there is no peace without justice, but peace goes beyond justice. Frequently 'peace' and 'righteousness' are bracketed together (Ps. 85.10; Isa. 48.18). After the exile, and the failure of the false prophets to bring a true word of peace (Ezek. 13.10, 16), the prophetic vision grows of a time when God's anointed king will bring in a new kingdom of righteous and just peace (Isa. 61.1ff.).

It is of interest to see how the Messianic figure in the various sections of the book of Isaiah is depicted as the bringer of peace. The figure is introduced as the coming King in Isaiah 9, and is described as ruling in peace. The ecological harmony of the vision of Isaiah 11, the wolf lying down with the lamb, the calf, the lion and the fatling together led by a little child, arises out of the rule of God's king with justice and righteousness. In the servant passages of the second part of Isaiah, the suffering servant brings peace to the people (53.5; 55.12) through his own costly self-giving. In the final sections, the Messianic figure now dons the garments of the conqueror who establishes peace by fighting for justice (cf. Isa. 59.8ff). The peaceable kingdom of *shalom* arises out of the rule of God, is established by the self-giving love of God, and depends on the victory of God over every injustice. *Shalom* – a vision of a sustainable community – means peace with justice.

Sustainability

It was the publication in 1987 of *Our Common Future*, the 'Brundtland' report from the United Nations World Commission on the Environment and Development, that has provided the most widely quoted definition of 'sustainable development': 'development that meets the needs of the present without compromising the ability of future generations to meet their own needs'.[5] There have, of course, been many different emphases

---

5 *Our Common Future*, 1987.

JUSTICE

given in the discussions about sustainability, but the basic assumption was the need for stewardship, and the fact that all nations and future generations are entitled to a share of the resources of the planet. As the WCC report *Solidarity with Victims of Climate Change* pointed out, however, subsequent discussions have not done justice to the challenge inherent in the concept of sustainability. People assumed that it was possible to work for sustainable development in the developing world while at the same time maintaining unchanged the economic system of the developed West. So the demands made on the planet continued unabated. Climate change has now forced on us the realization that greenhouse gas emissions at the current rate are making the whole planet unsustainable. If for no other reason, for the sake of our grandchildren, and the grandchildren of peoples around the world, we need to change. As the WCC report put it: 'For a society to be sustainable, scales of exploitation need to be respected. For justice to be achieved, limits to development must be set in the developed world. As long as these two requirements are not met, the degradation of life conditions is inevitable.'[6] In other words, the concept of 'sustainability' now needs to include the need to resist further degradation, and to increase the capacity to survive in deteriorating conditions; it needs to include a recognition that costly sacrifices will have to be made, especially in the Western developed world. Whether we like it or not, most realistic scenarios for carbon emissions reduction require us to make significant changes in lifestyle, not least from dependence on motorized mobility, and significantly to reduce flying, as well as carbon reduction in household use. Part of the background to climate change is that the Western industrialized societies have developed a pattern of life and consumption that is literally not sustainable.

---

6 WCC, *Solidarity*, p. 17.

Millennium development goals

In this context it is worth reminding ourselves of what came to be called the Millennium Development Goals, resolved at the General Assembly of the United Nations in September 2000.

The UN resolved by the year 2015 to achieve the following:

- to eradicate extreme poverty and hunger – to reduce by half the proportion of people living on less than one dollar a day; to reduce by half the proportion of people who suffer from hunger
- to achieve universal primary education – and ensure that all boys and girls complete a full course of primary schooling
- to promote gender equality and empower women – to ensure that girls have the same chance to receive education and be treated as fairly as boys in primary and secondary schools by 2005, and at all levels by 2015
- to reduce child mortality – to reduce by two-thirds the proportion of children dying before they are five years old
- to improve maternal health – and reduce by three-quarters the proportion of women dying as a result of having children
- to combat HIV/AIDS, malaria and other diseases – to halt and begin to reverse the spread of HIV/AIDS, the incidence of malaria and other major diseases
- to ensure environmental sustainability – to integrate the principles of sustainable development into country policies and programmes; to reverse the loss of environmental resources; to reduce by half the proportion of people without sustainable access to safe drinking water; to achieve significant improvement in the lives of at least 100 million slum dwellers by the year 2020
- to develop a global partnership for development, with targets for aid, trade and debt relief.

We can be thankful that some small progress has been made on some of these goals. But there is still an extremely long way to go, and the growing impacts of climate change – now viewed as significantly larger than when the Millennium Development Goals were formulated – is to make them less and less achievable without urgent and major changes in our priorities.

Climate change is already hitting the world's poorest communities more severely than the developed world. In one moment of television drama a member of the Inuit Community pleaded with some Western leaders, 'Do not destroy my world' – a world of Arctic ice which was melting around him. The distribution of the impacts of climate change are likely to be increasingly unjust, and to create new areas of growing vulnerability. This is because the changes in climate are uneven across the world. There may be some benefits of global warming in some more northern countries, such as some parts of Russia and the wheat-growing areas of Canada. The UK may benefit also, although should the ocean acidity change sufficiently for the Gulf Stream to be severely affected, the UK's temperature climate could become more severe, like central Europe.

But the poorer countries of the world have less resources or wealth, less capacity and power at present to cope with the demands of climate change, and so are less able to adapt than the richer parts of the world. Professor Richard Odingo, Vice-Chair of the Intergovernmental Panel on Climate Change, is quoted as saying: 'Climate change will make it impossible for the world to achieve the Millennium Development Goals. Poverty will increase. Food security is bound to get worse.'[7] It might be better expressed the other way round: 'Failing to meet the MDGs will make it impossible to live justly with a changing climate'. Amos's anger against the growing gap between the rich and the poor and the powerlessness of poverty has an extraordinarily modern ring.

One of the extremely valuable contributions of Christian Aid in recent years is to underline the fact that climate action is a matter of justice. Too often environmental issues and questions of development have been kept apart in the UK. That is not true

---

7 Quoted in Charles Reed's Church of England Briefing Paper, 'Climate Change is Not Just a Green Issue', August 2007.

elsewhere in the world. For example, David Gosling illustrates how in the developing world environmental questions are mostly experienced as integral to their social context.[8] In commenting on the Earth Summit of 1992, he notes that global warming that affects the rich nations was dealt with at Rio; desertification that affects the poor (e.g. the fact that the Sahara Desert is growing) was ignored.

Christian Aid has cogently argued that it is the poor of the world who are already suffering disproportionately from the effects of global warming, and that the potential effects of climate change could be so severe that they nullify efforts to secure sustainable development in poor countries. 'Climate change is a pressing poverty issue'.[9]

All this highlights the huge importance of trying to think and act in relation to sustainable development and to think and act in relation to care for the environment at the same time. Climate change, as we have emphasized, has converted climate into a justice issue. While the risks of climate reveal deep injustices, climate change does – or should – make us aware in fresh ways of these injustices and turn all climate risks into a justice issue. Climate justice is not simply about reducing carbon emissions – crucially important though that is; it is about not allowing the climate change agenda to obscure the major importance of issues of poverty in the world, and about requiring us to bring all these concerns together.

Opportunity

Climate change could thus present us with a unique opportunity as well as a threat. This could be the time when the industrialized world wakes up to the failure of the gods of consumption, and returns to 'Seek the Lord and live'. This could be the time when a recognition of the need to live within the rhythms of the natu-

---

8 David Gosling, *Religion and Ecology in India and South East Asia*, 2001.

9 Christian Aid, *The Climate of Poverty*.

ral world makes for the best for the health of the planet as well, therefore, as for human flourishing, and that we return to the moral and spiritual values for which God made us. This could be a time when the world comes together to work for climate justice – here and now – especially on behalf of the poorest. It is about poverty and trade justice here and now.

The changing climate is freshly revealing this dimension of injustice in the world in inescapable ways. The Scriptures hold out for us a vision of a sustainable covenant community within a sustainable world – of *shalom*, peace with justice, which touches all our relationships including to God and to the environment. Is that a vision around which all can work together?

Mitigation

The call to justice is a call to the governments of the world and to transnational corporations to act justly in relation to actions which need to be taken to mitigate the risks of dangerous climate change. Some of the crucial decisions concern the huge reductions in carbon emissions which will be needed to limit climate change to below dangerous levels. Many scientists are now calling for a reduction of emissions of 80% or more worldwide by the year 2050.[10] To achieve that fairly and justly requires considerable sacrifice in the developed world – among those who are likely to be reading this book – and considerable co-operation across the globe of a sort we have not so far seen.

The United Nations Framework Convention on Climate Change (UNFCCC) was set up in 1994 and has provided a start. At a subsequent meeting of representatives in Kyoto in 1997 a Protocol was negotiated and eventually after some years ratified by over 150 countries (but not the USA and Australia,

---

10 Cf. Kevin Anderson et al., 'Living within a carbon budget', a report from Tyndall Centre Manchester for Friends of the Earth and the Co-operative Bank, July 2006; www.tyndall.ac.uk/publication/briefing_notes/Livingwithacarbonbudget.pdf

though the latter signed up in autumn 2007). It required industrialized nations to agree to commit to reduce combined emissions by 5% from the 1990 level by 2008–12. Even these modest goals are unlikely to be reached, and it seems likely that developed nations will overshoot their Kyoto targets with a net increase of carbon emissions for the period 2008–12 of about 10% above 1990 levels.

Among the factors strangely omitted so far from international decisions on emission targets are aviation and international shipping. Aviation is the fastest growing sector in energy demand, and on present trends aviation will be the most significant energy consumer by 2050.

The United Nations held a summit conference in Bali in December 2007, to try to agree ways forward for the world beyond the Kyoto agreements which last until 2012. Although, disappointingly, Bali failed to agree to any enforceable targets for emissions reduction, largely because of the blocking tactics of the American delegation, it did provide a 'road map' for negotiations towards a further conference in Copenhagen in 2009, which should result in a post-Kyoto treaty to come into force in 2012. Bali's action plan, among other things:

- reaffirmed that 'economic and social development and poverty eradication are global priorities'
- recognized that deep cuts in global emissions will be required
- decided to work for international action on mitigation in the context of sustainable development
- pledged, among other things, to work for enhanced action on adaptation, 'taking into account the urgent and immediate needs of developing countries that are particularly vulnerable to the adverse effects of climate change', risk management, disaster-reduction strategies, and enhanced action on the development of environmentally sound technologies
- agreed that the process shall be informed by the best available scientific information.[11]

---

11 Bali Action Plan.

Contraction and convergence

One of the models which have been proposed to attempt to achieve the UNFCCC objectives is called 'Contraction and Convergence'. This seems to have received a good deal of international support. It is not without its critics, but seems to offer a good model towards a just and fair approach to mitigation.

The approach was devised in 2000 by Aubrey Meyer, and is based on carbon rationing. At the moment, the rate of greenhouse gas emissions are hugely uneven across the planet. The model starts by proposing a global 'budget' for carbon emission targeted at a safe and stable future level. Then the permitted amount of carbon per person on the globe is calculated, which gives each country a figure for its allowable emissions. So international 'shares' in this budget are agreed, as well as a plan for gradually diminishing the amount of greenhouse gases that the world can emit in each year for the coming century. The idea would be that the world would 'converge' towards the situation when the same amount of carbon could be emitted by each person on the planet – which means that some of the poorer countries could emit more than they do at present, and the richer countries would need significantly to reduce their emissions to ensure an overall progressive contraction worldwide. Amounts of carbon could be traded between countries, with carbon credits bought and sold between richer and poorer countries. The proposed model assumes that on this basis, overall greenhouse gas emissions are likely to rise until about 2020, but after that could start significantly to fall until by the year 2100 they would be back to about the 1980s' level. This model is an attempt to create fairness between nations, based on the principle that 'the polluter pays'.

There is a danger in this approach, however, in that it can be interpreted in terms of 'rights to pollute' leading to 'pollution permits' and the sort of carbon trading which makes pollution another sort of economic activity.[12] If we are not careful, we

---

12 Although sulphur dioxide emissions in the USA were subject to trading schemes in the 1980s/1990s, and did make a difference.

could be back to the priority of the consumer market economy, with carbon trading leading to another sort of injustice: one rich country buys carbon from a poor country, enabling the rich to sustain their lifestyle and continue developing and continue polluting, while the gap between rich and poor grows wider.

There is an alternative model supported by Christian Aid, called the Greenhouse Development Rights (GDR) approach. This seeks justice in the sharing out of the burdens of restricting carbon emissions. It offers a fair and transparent means of sharing out the burden, and is based on responsibility for the problem and the capability to deal with its consequences, rather than on the concept of the 'right to pollute'. The focus is on 'development rights', and a clear linkage of the tasks of reducing carbon emissions with the tasks of sustainable development.[13]

What about India and China?

Many people are worried about the two fastest growing economies, India and China. A very common question that is asked in discussions of actions needed to mitigate climate change is, 'What about India and China?' One of the reasons why the US and Australia refused to sign up to the Kyoto Protocol was that it did not require India and China to take action to reduce their emissions before 2012. But the reality is that India and China currently emit a lesser amount of carbon dioxide per person compared to the emissions per person in the USA and other Western countries.

Al Gore compares the per capita carbon emissions in Africa, India and China (all below the world average, but growing) with Japan, the European Union and Russia (all between two and three times the world average) and the United States (between five and six times the world average).[14] Clearly the populations of India and China are growing rapidly, and the amount of their emissions is growing fast. Many of the Chinese

---

13 Christian Aid, *Truly Inconvenient*, 2007.
14 Gore, *An Inconvenient Truth*, p. 253.

factories are, of course, producing goods to be sold in Western markets. The time will come soon when China greatly exceeds the United States in pollution, but the important issues here are the right of the developing world to develop to the extent that the Western world has already done, and the share of responsibility the Western world must take to help clean up the energy supplies in the developing world.

The Western world has had 200 years to develop to its present state of industrialization, has been the main polluter and contributed most significantly to the present levels of carbon dioxide in the atmosphere. China and India are trying to reach equivalent levels of development within a generation. Their reluctance to agree to emissions targets is understandable until the rich West – and America (responsible for 25% of global greenhouse gas emission) in particular – has taken significant action. With several new coal-fired power stations being built every month in China, development of technologies to reduce emissions from them (such as carbon capture and storage[15]) is clearly urgent.

Adaptation

The task is also to find just and fair ways of *adapting* to the climate change that is already inevitable. We know that the climate will continue to change, even if we were to cease all carbon emissions. The Tyndall Centre for Climate Change Research at the University of East Anglia has for some while been addressing the question of the justice implications of adaptation. The issue has many aspects to it, and their careful work demonstrates the complexity of the questions and that there are no simplistic answers.

What are the potential barriers to adaptation that may limit the ability of societies to adapt to climate change? What are the

---

15 The process whereby carbon dioxide is not released into the atmosphere but 'captured' and stored safely underground.

boundaries in physical and ecological systems beyond which it is not feasible for societies to adapt? How is adaptation possible if the change occurring is irreversible? Where do we draw lines in seeking to preserve habitats or particular ecosystems or to prevent the extinction of certain species? (How do we, for example, weigh human values against the needs of other aspects of God's creation?) It is clear that values and culture underpin how different societies perceive and interpret the world, and this will influence the decisions they make about adaptation to climate change. (What, for example, would the irreversible loss of a particular cultural heritage mean to a society? Where should the Inuit man, whose home was melting, go? How would he feed his family? There was no chance of his children continuing in the Inuit culture, and yet to move would be a major loss of place, and of identity. How do the impacts of climate change vary from one culture to another? I may choose not to fly in an aircraft. The peasant farmer in north-east India has no such choice. He is powerless to make such a decision: his one goal is to feed his family today.) How are the potential values of future generations to be included in our decisions about adaptation? How do our different ways of knowing about the world influence our decisions? What implications are there of different forms of government being involved in global decisions?

As Adger and his co-authors say, 'global collective action is needed to prevent potentially catastrophic impacts of our unprecedented experiment with the planetary climate system and to adapt to unavoidable climate change.'[16] They go on to argue that the distribution of climate change impacts is likely to continue to be unjust, and to create new vulnerabilities which will also be unfair. The goal of the UNFCCC is to stabilize greenhouse gases 'at a level and within a timeframe that makes it possible for natural ecosystems, food production systems, and economic systems to adapt'. It also establishes a duty on the developed countries to assist vulnerable developing countries in

---

16 Adger et al. (eds), *Fairness*, p. 1.

JUSTICE

adapting to climate change and in meeting the costs of adaptation. Adger and his co-authors argue that there are four crucial elements which would take us a step further towards climate justice:

- an acceptance of responsibility for climate change impacts
- the duty to assist vulnerable developing countries to adapt
- the principle of putting the most vulnerable first
- the principle of universal participation.[17]

As they conclude, 'Politics and law can ultimately have no higher purpose than seeking fair outcomes for the survival of the natural world.'[18]

It is part of the task of the Christian Church to bear prophetic witness to governments and transnational corporations holding before them the divine requirement of justice in all human affairs, and therefore such questions as the responsibility of developed countries for the impacts of climate change elsewhere in the world; the assistance developed countries should give to developing countries; and how the burden of assistance can fairly be shared and decisions fairly made.[19]

There are, of course, many other factors which relate to poverty, development and climate justice, and I simply note three more of them here.

Other related issues

Population

One important issue is that of voluntary population control. When Christ was born, the world population was under 250 million people. One hundred years ago it was under 2,000 million. It took 10,000 generations to reach two billion; it took

---

17 Adger et al. (eds), *Fairness*, p. 19.
18 Adger et al. (eds), *Fairness*, p. 19.
19 Adger et al. (eds), *Fairness*.

one generation to double it. Now it is over 6,500 million and is predicted to rise to about 9,000 million by 2050. There is a link between population growth and poverty.

As Professor John Guillebaud, Emeritus Professor of Family Planning and Reproductive Health in London, put it, 'The annual increment of over 75 million humans per year (all births minus all deaths on the entire planet) equates to a city for one million persons having to be built, somewhere, every five days.'[20] This increase is chiefly happening in the developing world, in Africa, India, China – using more earth, and creating more greenhouse gases, and putting more pressure on the life support systems of the planet.

'Climate change is very much linked to the number of climate *changers*!' The implications of this are wide. Guillebaud argues that by 2025 our species will have taken over so much of the earth that an estimated one-fifth of all the world's other life forms will be eliminated through habitat destruction. And though birth rates are declining, the population – and therefore poverty – will continue to grow for some while. 'All of tomorrow's parents are already born, so many in number that if their average family sizes were improbably to average two, population growth (despite the ravages of AIDS) would not cease until around 9–10 billion.' Nine billion people will require two planets to sustain them on current world average consumption trends, and the cycle of population growth leading to more poverty leading to higher population growth becomes an increasingly vicious one.

Guillebaud rightly argues that Christians should be enthusiastic supporters of voluntary birth planning worldwide. 'Reducing unplanned pregnancies, an incremental reduction in average family sizes, fewer to share the "cake" of the family's resources, hence less poverty, more children surviving so more acceptance of smaller family size through family planning and ultimately less population growth.' He says that without adequate birth

---

20 J. Guillebaud, 'Population Growth, Global Warming and Sustainability of the Environment', in *The Bible in Transmission*, 2006.

planning, delivered wisely and compassionately, our human numbers 'will exceed the carrying capacity of the land available'. On my visits to Zambia and South Africa with Christian Aid a few years ago I met a number of people working at clinics supporting people with AIDS. They would strongly endorse Guillebaud's plea for more adequate education about family planning and the provision of contraceptive advice and resources. A changing climate and a growing population are not unrelated: more people means more carbon dioxide, just as more people means more poverty.

Deforestation

A further factor in global warming is the loss of forests. For some centuries many countries have been clearing forest land to make way for agriculture. And this is not simply a question for far-off countries. The British Colonial Government in India in the 1860s devastated forests to build ships, supply sleepers for railways, manufacture paper and furniture; this led to the breakdown of co-operatives and local community initiatives among people who had traditionally had free access to the forests for their needs.[21] Trade and economics are important drivers of deforestation. John Houghton indicates that at the global level 'the net loss in forest area during the 1990s was an estimated 940,000 square kilometers' (that is more than nine times the size of Ireland). This has a huge effect on land degradation, on loss of bio-diversity, on rainfall and, without the trees to absorb carbon dioxide from the atmosphere, a huge effect also on carbon emissions and thus on global warming. Houghton argues that 'Reducing deforestation can make a substantial contribution to slowing the increase of greenhouse gases in the atmosphere' and, indeed, that planting new forests would also make a substantial improvement.[22]

---

21 Gosling, *Religion and Ecology*.
22 Houghton, *Global Warming*, pp. 249ff.

The 2007 UN Bali Conference acknowledged the contribution of deforestation to global anthropogenic greenhouse gas emissions.[23] Among other things, it

- affirmed the urgent need to take further meaningful action to reduce emissions from deforestation and forest degradation
- encouraged all parties to support capacity-building, facilitate the transfer of technology to improve such things as data collection and estimation of emissions from deforestation
- addressed the institutional needs of developing countries to reduce emissions from deforestation.

The Conference clearly noted the impact of deforestation on climate change and requires the future treaty to include provision to aid countries severely to reduce this practice.

Economic reforms

The Lambeth bishops called for governments and transnational corporations to 'bring about economic reforms which will establish a just and fair trading system both for people and for the environment'.

There is a huge ideological debate, beyond the scope of this book, about the extent to which capitalism, and the consumer culture to which it leads, is not only the major contributor to our current climate crisis, but also could be the route towards its solution. On the one hand, many environmentalists see capitalism as the major evil. Such a view is developed from a theological perspective in Michael Northcott's *A Moral Climate*. Northcott links the moral issues raised by climate change to the foundations of the modern global economy. Where did our dependence on fossil fuel come from? It is related to the philosophical and economic thinking which gave rise to the free market.

---

23 There was explicit recognition of REDD (Reduced Emissions from Deforestation and Degradation in Developing Countries), under which countries reducing their deforestation rates would receive payments from an international fund supported by donor country contributions.

JUSTICE

> At the heart of the present crisis is . . . the global market empire fashioned by the United States and Europe in the last fifty years, as governments have deregulated money and trade and freed up economic actors and financial markets to enable maximal wealth accumulation by banks and corporations without regard to political sovereignty or territorial limits . . . Global warming is the earth's judgement on the global market empire and on the heedless consumption it fosters.[24]

Addressing the long-term problems of climate change, he argues, will require 'reductions in economic growth in the Western world, a reining in of corporate greed and the re-regulation of the money supply'. Many environmentalists argue the need for the collapse of global capitalism before environmental progress can be made.

A different perspective is found in Jonathan Porritt's book *Capitalism as if the World Matters*. Porritt, environmental campaigner and Chair of the UK government's Sustainable Development Commission, would agree with Northcott up to a point. Unbridled capitalism is the source of our problems. However, in the political world in which we now live, change in the timescale needed will only be achieved through the structures we have – namely, through the instruments of price, market and exchange. Porritt therefore argues for a reformed capitalism as part of the solution. Even though inherited capitalism is largely responsible for the threats of dangerous climate change, the depletion of resources, extinction of some species, and growing gaps between rich and poor, it is possible to develop an alternative model, a 'capitalism as if the world matters'[25] which could sustain our ecosystems and still allow businesses to grow. Porritt then explores what a more sustainable planet and society could look like, and focuses more on well-being than consumer goods. He builds on the core values of interdependence, equity, responsibility and justice – not far, in fact, from

---

24 Northcott, *A Moral Climate*, pp. 5, 7.
25 Jonathon Porritt, *Capitalism as if the World Matters*, 2005.

the concerns of the prophet Amos. There is a significant Christian task still to be done to contribute to the political and economic dimensions of this debate.

Justice also applies, of course, at all other levels of our human relationships. The Church's engagement with local authorities; the Church's own lifestyle and priorities, and individual Christians in their personal and family lives are called to live by the prophet Micah's call to 'do justice, and to love kindness, and to walk humbly with your God', and to Amos's plea to 'Seek the Lord and live'. I will explore some of these further dimensions to Christian allegiance to the Lord in the final chapter on the gift and calling of the covenant people of God.

6

Redemption: covenant hope

> Great is the mystery of faith:
> Christ has died,
> Christ is risen,
> Christ will come again.
>
> Common Worship, Holy Communion

In the Rijksmuseum in Amsterdam hangs one of the most famous of Rembrandt's earlier works, painted in 1630. It is called *Jeremiah lamenting the destruction of Jerusalem*, and depicts the prophet Jeremiah with a sorrowful face lined with wrinkles and covered with a white beard, melancholically resting his head on his hand. His elbow is propped on a large book. Around him are various precious vessels, perhaps from the temple.

The date is 587 BC. Exiles from the kingdom of Judah are being taken away to Babylon. Away in the far distance in the painting, Jerusalem is being plundered by Nebuchadnezzar's troops and Judah's King Zedekiah, blinded by the invading soldiers, is covering his eyes. It is the scene Jeremiah had been warning against for all of his long ministry. The book presumably represents the Book of the Law, which had been the basis of the reforms of good King Josiah who was a contemporary of Jeremiah in his younger days. The young king was aware of the political unrest in the region, that the northern kingdom of Israel had been brought to an end and that his kingdom of Judah was effectively a vassal of the mighty Assyria. The early chapters of Jeremiah's prophecy depict a people enmeshed in pagan worship and immorality. Josiah sought the Lord, and began a programme of reform, trying to purge the country of idolatry. The discovery of a forgotten book of the law, which many people identify with Deuteronomy, gave to King Josiah – and also the prophet Jeremiah – a firm basis on which to call the people back to their covenant God, and their covenant obligations. For Jeremiah, as for Amos and other prophets 200 years earlier, God's judgement was falling on the people of God because they had broken his covenant and turned from his ways.

Jeremiah reflects on the miseries of his time, both of the people and of the environment, and sees in them a sign of God's judgement.

> 'Disaster overtakes disaster, the whole land is laid waste ... My people are foolish, they do not know me; ... they are skilled in doing evil, but do not know how to do good.' I looked on the earth, and lo, it was waste and void; and to the heavens and they had no light. I looked on the mountains, and lo, they were quaking, and all the hills moved to and fro. I looked, and lo, there was no one at all, and all the birds of the air had fled. I looked, and lo, the fruitful land was a desert, and all its cities were laid in ruins before the LORD, before his fierce anger. (Jer. 4.23–24)

And more explicitly:

> Do you not fear me? says the LORD: Do you not tremble before me? I placed the sand as a boundary for the sea, a perpetual barrier that it cannot pass; though the waves toss, they cannot prevail, though they roar, they cannot pass over it. But this people has a stubborn and rebellious heart; they have turned aside and gone away. They do not say in their hearts, 'Let us fear the LORD our God, who give the rain in its season, the autumn rain and the spring rain, and keeps for us the weeks appointed for the harvest.' Your iniquities have turned these away, and your sins have deprived you of good. (Jer. 5.22–23)

REDEMPTION: COVENANT HOPE

The sense here is not of God vindictively withholding rainfall in order to punish a disobedient people, but that the breaking of the covenant between God and his people inevitably has repercussions for all the other covenanted relationships his people were part of – with each other and with their environment. It is the Deuteronomic theme again: where there is commitment to God and walking in God's ways, there is the blessing of fruitfulness; refusal to walk in God's ways leads to consequences which can affect the environment, even the climate.

This is how Jeremiah interprets a time of drought:

> Judah mourns and her gates languish; they lie in gloom on the ground, and the cry of Jerusalem goes up. Her nobles send their servants for water; they come to the cisterns, they find no water, they return with their vessels empty. They are ashamed and cover their heads, because the ground is cracked. Because there has been no rain on the land the farmers are dismayed; they cover their heads. Even the doe in the field forsakes her newborn fawn because there is no grass. The wild asses stand on the bare heights, they pant for air like jackals; their eyes fail because there is no herbage. (Jer. 14.1–6)

On this poignant passage about lack of water, Derek Kidner comments, 'In a few terrible verses, the plight of every living thing confronts us – for lack of what none can command, and none can do without. On so fine a thread hangs all we take for granted.'[1]

Human actions have consequences for the whole of our ecosystem: the precariousness and interconnectedness of all life is underlined. Human sin affects the planet.

Many years earlier than Jeremiah, Isaiah of Jerusalem had similarly linked changes in the earth through changes in the climate with human sinfulness and the breaking of God's covenant:

---

[1] Derek Kidner, *The Message of Jeremiah*, 1987.

> The earth dries up and withers, the world languishes and withers; the heavens languish together with the earth. The earth lies polluted under its inhabitants; for they have transgressed laws, violated statutes, broken the everlasting covenant. (Isa. 24.4–5)

This is another example of the moral and spiritual dimensions to the relationship between humanity and our environment – and so to the climate. Ultimately, the crisis of climate change will not be solved simply by technology or economics. Of course, we will need to use the very best science and technology available. Of course, there will need to be agreed political and economic decisions. But the crisis goes much deeper. The deeper question is who we are, and what human living on this earth means and can mean. Climate change takes us back to questions of God, creation and human covenant-breaking. Fundamentally, climate change is a moral and spiritual question.

We need to go back again to the earliest creation story in Genesis 2 and 3 to set the context for this understanding of the ecological implications of human sin.

Genesis 2 and 3

As we have seen, the Genesis narrative in these two chapters tells the story of human ambiguity. There is a garden with trees that are pleasant to the sight and good for food; there is water and refreshment; there is freedom and delight. Humanity, male and female, is given the responsibility of serving and protecting the garden, which is a home both for plants and animals, and is the human social context for personal love. But the paradox of human freedom is the need for boundaries to prevent liberty becoming destructive licence. The boundary in the garden is the provision of the one tree – of the knowledge of good and evil – from which human beings were not to eat. Humanity was intended to grow in the knowledge of God on the basis of obedience to God's word. But as Genesis 3 so graphically illustrates, by some inscrutable providence, a voice of temptation comes from within the garden casting doubt on the reliability of God's word, and enticing humanity to 'be like God'.

That reaching across God-given boundaries is the basis of what Christian theology calls sin. It shows itself in regarding humanity and the world as autonomous, and without need of God. It leads to what St Paul calls worshipping and serving the creature, rather than the Creator (Rom. 1.25). In the garden, temptation prepares the way for disobedience. The man and the woman experience the power of wrong in their lives. Their eyes are opened; they now know something of good and evil. And so the narrative expounds the anatomy of human sin: obedience gives way to rebellion; openness gives way to shame; responsible living is coloured by guilt; freedom is replaced by bondage; blessing becomes curse; sexual complementarity becomes subordination; work is experienced as toil; human fellowship is replaced by banishment from the garden; the gift of life becomes the rule of death.[2]

'Cursed is the ground'

Among the effects of God's reaction to human sin in the story in Genesis 3, is his 'curse' of the ground:

> Cursed is the ground because of you; in toil you shall eat of it all the days of your life; thorns and thistles it shall bring forth for you; and you shall eat the plants of the field. By the sweat of your face you shall eat bread until you return to the ground, for out of it you were taken; you are dust, and to dust you shall return. (Gen. 3.17–18)

What is this? Cassuto comments on Gen. 3.17 that in order to understand the nature of the earth's 'curse' we must first understand what is meant by its 'blessing'. He cites Deut. 33.13–15 to show that a blessed land is one that is amply watered and fertile – so, he says, a cursed land lacks water and

---

2 Cf. Atkinson, *The Message of Genesis 1–11*, Chapter 2.

fertility.³ In the garden, which was well watered and produced abundant fruit, human beings were able to live with satisfaction and without anxiety. From then on, however, the earth would yield its harvest only with difficulty and struggle.

Von Rad writes of a break in the 'affectionate relationship' between human beings and the earth, which is the material basis for life – that is, the 'solidarity' of creation which existed between human beings and the earth is now broken. There is 'an alienation that expresses itself in a silent, dogged struggle between man and the soil'.⁴

In summary, God's curse of the ground is another way of expressing the fact that the relationship of human beings to the environment is fractured through human sin. The symbol of that fracture is the Genesis reference to 'thorns and thistles'.

It is clear that many of the factors contributing to climate change reflect the efforts of human beings in different ways to reach out beyond God-given boundaries, to refuse to live within the terms of God's covenant of peace. So Michael Northcott writes of the 'threatened collapse of industrial civilisation' as traceable to 'an imperious refusal of biopolitical limits' and the 'refusal of modern humans to see themselves as creatures, contingently embedded in networks of relationships with other creatures, and with the Creator'.⁵

It is that fracture in the relationship between human beings and their environment – and indeed with each other – which is the result of the fracture of humanity's relationship with the Creator God of the cosmic covenant, which forms the backdrop for the whole covenant story of the redemption of God's people Israel, and through them of all humanity and God's world.

The covenant story beginning with God's call to Abraham, and worked out through Moses, David, the Deuteronomic historian and the prophets, is told as the response of the Creator God to his people, through the gift of the covenant of redemp-

---

3 U. Cassuto, *A Commentary on the Book of Genesis*, 1961.
4 G. von Rad, *Genesis: A Commentary*, p. 91.
5 Northcott, *A Moral Climate*, pp. 5, 16.

REDEMPTION: COVENANT HOPE

tion. The calling of Abraham is God's response to the sins of Adam. It is worked out as the promise of a new people, Israel, who would be called to serve as a light to all humanity. The covenant of redemption is God's response to human failing. It begins in God's steadfast, faithful love, as perhaps most clearly seen in the prophecy of Hosea, who describes the character of the covenant Lord in terms of God's steadfast, faithful love (Hebrew: *chesed*). The covenant obligation on God's people, and so on all humanity, is then to respond with a commitment of steadfast, faithful, loving allegiance. There are times of blessing and fruitfulness; there are times of failure, judgement and drought.

The broken covenant calls for radical renewal

It is significant that Amos, who so clearly denounced the people of God for their covenant failures, also eventually held out a hope of restoration.

> The time is surely coming, says the LORD, when the one who ploughs shall overtake the one who reaps, and the treader of grapes the one who sows the seed; the mountains shall drip sweet wine, and all the hills shall flow with it. I will restore the fortunes of my people Israel, and they shall rebuild the ruined cities and inhabit them; they shall plant vineyards and drink their wine, and they shall make gardens and eat their fruit. (Amos 9.13f.)

> Likewise, his southern contemporary, Isaiah of Jerusalem, looks for the time when 'the wilderness and the dry land shall be glad, the desert shall rejoice and blossom; like the crocus it shall blossom abundantly, and rejoice with joy and singing' (Isa. 35.1f.).

It is 150 years later, however, throughout most of the second part of Isaiah – that is, chapters 40–55 – that the vision of renewal and restoration is most fully elaborated. Comforting words to the people of God in exile in Babylon hold out the vision of a people living under God's pardon and in God's peace, in which even thorns and thistles are replaced:

> You shall go out in joy and be led back in peace; the mountains and the hills before you shall burst into song, and all the trees of the field shall clap their hands. Instead of the thorn shall come up the cypress; instead of the brier shall come up the myrtle; and it shall be to the LORD for a memorial, for an everlasting sign that shall not be cut off. (Isa. 55.12f.)

Ezekiel has a vision of the dry bones in the valley coming back to life, ending with a renewed covenant promise:

> I will make a covenant of peace with them; it shall be an everlasting covenant with them; and I will bless them and multiply them, and will set my sanctuary among them for evermore. (Ezek. 37.26)

But it is to Jeremiah, with whose lamentations we began this chapter, that we turn for the richest promise of a renewed covenant.

> The days are surely coming, says the LORD, when I will make a new covenant with the house of Israel and the house of Judah. It will not be like the covenant that I made with their ancestors when I took them by the hand to bring them out of the land of Egypt – a covenant that they broke, though I was their husband, say the LORD. But this is the covenant that I will make with the house of Israel after those days, says the LORD: I will put my law within them, and I will write it on their hearts; and I will be their God, and they shall be my people. (Jer. 31.31f.)

The sacrifice of the servant

What is the basis for this renewal of the covenant, for this hope of restoration and renewal? It is again derived from the character of God, the Creator God, who is described by Isaiah as both Saviour and 'the Redeemer of Israel' (Isa. 49.7):

REDEMPTION: COVENANT HOPE

But now, thus says the LORD, he who created you, O Jacob, he who formed you, O Israel: Do not fear, for I have redeemed you; I have called you by name, you are mine. When you pass through the waters, I will be with you; and through the rivers, they shall not overwhelm you; when you walk through fire you shall not be burned, and the flame shall not consume you. For I am the LORD your God, the Holy One of Israel, your Saviour. (Isa. 43.1f.)

In this remarkable passage, the logic of what is going on is rooted in God's covenanted love and faithfulness. 'It means that Yahweh even goes with the people in the floods and fires of Yahweh's own punishment that the people are currently experiencing . . . Yahweh's own presence will actually neutralize the forces of destruction that Yahweh unleashed.'[6]

The Lord (Yahweh) acts to demonstrate his faithfulness and commitment to his people and his world, even when the failures of his people have ended up with them in exile.

As Isaiah develops his prophecy in chapters 40–55, the figure of a Servant of the Lord emerges as the coming One through whom the Creator God's saving and redeeming and restoring is brought about. In a series of changing images, a picture finally emerges of the Suffering Servant who offers himself to the Lord. Goldingay comments, 'This would compensate for the massive affront to Yahweh constituted by the people's rebellious life in which they would not submit themselves to serve Yahweh and therefore made themselves liable to the suffering they experienced.'[7] Creation and covenant are woven together. It is the Creator God (Isaiah 40) that answers the cry of the exiles; and the God of the covenant who promises comfort and redemption in accordance with his covenant faithfulness, or (we may translate), justice.

The heart of the Suffering Servant's gift is self-sacrifice. In many ways, of course, the concept of sacrifice – in the sense of

---

6 Goldingay, *Isaiah*.
7 Goldingay, *Isaiah*.

the laying down of life that others may live – is at the heart of the whole biological process. Organic life develops through suffering. Some new life cannot come into being without death. The food chain is at the same time destructive of life and life-giving. There is a principle of vicarious suffering whereby new life is achieved only by sacrifice. Even Harry Potter discovered that! The natural rhythms of death and new life in the plant kingdom and the death of the antelope as food for the lion in their different ways show the paradox of sacrifice in the natural world. Life laid down is the source of new life.

But the natural biological processes point towards richer meanings at a higher level in the human world, namely, the meaning of suffering, and the meaning of self-giving love. The Suffering Servant of Isaiah 53, who for Christians has become understood as pointing towards Jesus Christ as God's Messiah, exemplifies a sacrificial suffering through to something higher, fuller, more whole. The great chapter of redemption in Isaiah 55 speaks again of the 'everlasting covenant' which is seen in God's forgiveness and providence, refreshing rain and fruitful earth, and joy and *shalom* for which the mountains and hill burst into song and the trees clap their hands. The cypress grows instead of the thorns, the myrtle instead of the brier. The 'curse' of Genesis 3 is replaced by a promise that the land will be renewed, and that renewal 'shall be to the LORD for a memorial, for an everlasting sign' (Isa. 55.13) – in other words, that God's restored land will not be devastated again. The New Testament picks up all these themes. In Christ, God suffers to achieve a renewed and restored life for his people. Redemptive suffering, which is at the heart of Isaiah 53, is also at the heart of the Christian Gospel in the New Testament, centred on Jesus Christ, God's Servant King.

The suffering Christ, and his resurrection

It is the first chapter of the letter to the Colossians which most vividly links Jesus Christ both to the creation, and to the

REDEMPTION: COVENANT HOPE

covenant of redemption seen in the suffering of his Cross, and his now exalted state as the risen Lord:

> He is the image of the invisible God, the first born of all creation; for in him all things in heaven and on earth were created, things visible and invisible . . . all things have been created through him and for him. He himself is before all things, and in him all things hold together. He is the head of the body, the church . . . in him all the fullness of God was pleased to dwell, and through him God was pleased to reconcile to himself all things, whether on earth or in heaven, by making peace through the blood of his cross. (Col. 1.15f.)

Remarkably, here, St Paul (or whoever was responsible for writing this poem) argues that the risen and exalted Jesus is the agent of God in creation, and has become the one in whom now all things hold together. But even more: it is through the crucified and risen Lord Jesus that all things, all people, all creatures, all creation, are restored into God's purposes. Here is a vision of the cosmic Christ, and also a vision of a new creation. What has been fractured through humanity's sin in our relationship with the created order, can, in St Paul's vision, here be put right.

The New Testament describes Jesus Christ, through whom all things were made, in terms both of the fulfillment of God's promise to Abraham, and as the climax of God's covenanted promises to Israel. St Paul understands faith in Jesus as bringing people into the family of faith which began with Abraham. He describes the way in which the understanding of God's law which was dimly understood in the time of Moses is transposed into the clarity and freedom of the Spirit of Jesus Christ. He sees Jesus as born in the line of David. In fact, Jesus Christ is 'the son of David, the son of Abraham' (Matt. 1.1.).

In Jesus, creation and covenant belong together. Jesus is the first born and the agent of creation. He is also the 'head of his Body, the church'; he is the one in whom the Christian Church as God's covenant community finds its being. Thus St Paul in

Galatians 3–4 speaks of all those baptized into Jesus Christ as 'all children of God through faith' (3.26). Later in the same letter he writes of the Christian Church as 'the Israel of God' (6.16). This corresponds with St Matthew's designation of the 12 apostles as 'judging the twelve tribes of Israel' in the new world, at the 'renewal of all things when the Son of Man is seated on the throne of his glory' (Matt. 18.28ff.). In other words, as Jesus, the Suffering Servant, represents both God's people Israel, and through them the whole of humanity, so Jesus the risen and exalted Lord represents the people of God's new covenant – the Church – and is in himself what true humanity was meant to be.

The Church, then, is God's new people. In Adam all die, in Christ all may be made alive. 'The Church rises on Easter morning in place of the Israel that has died on the cross: and all who want to belong to the reconstituted people of God must be joined to the Messiah, by baptism and faith, in his death and resurrection.'[8]

That is not to say that the Christian Church already fully demonstrates the humanity which Christ came to liberate. We are still in a world under judgement, infected by sin, in need of healing. But the promise of God's new people in God's new world comes with the eruption of God's kingly rule into the world in the life, death and resurrection of Jesus Christ. The Church is called to witness to the Lord obediently, living by his grace shown especially in the Word and Sacraments, waiting and working – with pain and struggle, sometimes – for the time when that kingly rule comes in all its fullness in the kingdom of Christ's glory. And that waiting and struggling is true also of the whole created order.

The suffering creation, and its hope

St Paul develops this theme in his letter to the Romans. At the climax of his detailed argument, he writes:

---

8 N.T. Wright, *Evangelical Anglican Identity*, 1980, pp. 15f.

REDEMPTION: COVENANT HOPE

I consider that the sufferings of this present time are not worth comparing with the glory about to be revealed to us. For creation waits with eager longing for the revealing of the children of God; for the creation was subjected to futility, not of its own will but by the will of the one who subjected it, in hope that the creation itself will be set free from its bondage to decay and will obtain the freedom of the glory of the children of God. We know that the whole creation has been groaning in labour pains until now; and not only the creation, but we ourselves, who have the first fruits of the Spirit, groan inwardly while we wait for adoption, the redemption of our bodies. For in hope we were saved. Now hope that is seen is not hope. For who hopes for what is seen? But if we hope for what we do not see, we wait for it with patience. (Rom. 8.18f.)

The first thing to notice about this text is that in Paul's view, creation is 'waiting', 'subjected to futility' and 'groaning', and the sufferings of the present time are like the 'labour pains' of someone waiting for a new birth. In other words, in God's purposes, the whole of creation is expectant in its struggles and sufferings that a new freedom will be obtained. Secondly, the redemption of creation is linked to the redemption ('revealing', 'adoption', 'glory') of the children of God.

To bring these different aspects of Paul's thought together, in Jesus, the crucified, risen and exalted Lord, God has acted to redeem the world – and that means not simply humanity, but the whole created order. Speaking of the Kingdom of God, glimpsed and promised in Jesus, Oliver O'Donovan wrote, 'In the resurrection of Christ, creation is restored and the kingdom of God dawns'.[9] Hans Küng put it this way: 'God's kingdom is creation healed.'[10]

A related train of thought can be found in the great theologian of the second century, Irenaeus. Irenaeus is very clear that God

---
9 O.M.T. O'Donovan *Resurrection and Moral Order*, 1988, p. 15.
10 H. Küng, *On Being a Christian*, tr. Edward Quinn, 1977, p. 231.

is not creation: only God *is*, everything else *exists* by virtue of God's creative power. For Irenaeus, creation is itself an incarnation of the Word and Spirit of God. Jesus Christ is the incarnate Son of God who is 'God made visible'. Christ's humanity makes divinity available to our perception. We receive in Christ what we lost in Adam: that is, being in the image and likeness of God. God's kingdom is the process whereby God fashions his creation and his creatures into his image and likeness – so Adam is a 'type' of Christ, and Christ became what we are in order to make us what he is. It is only after the resurrection of God's people that the intermingling of matter and Spirit in God's earth-creature (us) becomes fully again the image and likeness of God. 'Between the manifestation of this mingling of earthly and spiritual in the incarnation and its realization in their own bodies at the resurrection, the bodies of believers are sustained and prepared by that mingling of flesh and Spirit which is the body and blood of Christ in the Eucharist.' One day, says Irenaeus, there will be a new heaven and a new earth, and God will be all and in all and the everlasting reign of the Father will begin.[11]

The hope of the Christian to share in the resurrection of Christ, to share in the life of God's kingdom in its fullness, is also the hope that the whole of the created order will be reborn, renewed and healed. St Matthew's Gospel refers to the 'new creation', or 'the renewal of all things' (19.28). The second letter of Peter speaks of the present heavens and earth being 'preserved for fire, being kept until the day of judgment' (v. 7), and of the heavens being 'set ablaze and dissolved, and the elements [melting]' with fire (v. 12). Although this has sometimes been interpreted in terms of the disappearance of this world altogether, and therefore to remove any rationale for preserving the earth, the context is one of divine judgement through the sort of fire which purifies and reconstitutes: 'then the heavens will pass away with a loud noise, and the elements will be dissolved with fire, *and the earth and everything that is done on it will be disclosed*' (v. 10). It is then that Peter writes of 'a new

---

11 Cf. Denis Minns, *Irenaeus*, 1994.

heavens and a new earth, where righteousness is at home' (2 Pet. 3.13).

In such references much of the vision of the prophets of the Old Testament comes to its fulfilment in the kingdom of the risen and exalted Lord Jesus. And that vision is not only of individual people coming to faith and living as separate disciples. The vision is of a new community, a new covenant people, a new humanity, co-workers together (cf. Col. 4.11), whose faithfulness and obedience is the means by which God redeems and heals all things. And the centre of that future is Jesus Christ who, we read in the letter to the Ephesians, is the one in whom God gathers up *all things* – things in heaven and things on earth (Eph. 1.10). Such a vision does not imply a naïve optimism that 'everything will work out'. It is no guarantee that sinful human beings will get it all right about population growth, deforestation, energy use, biodiversity. Such a vision does not rule out future catastrophes if humanity continues to misuse God's earth. But, as the psalmist said, even in death, God is 'renewing the face of the earth', and the vision of God's kingdom is ultimately of 'creation healed'.

A new heaven and a new earth

The first time we read of 'a new heaven and a new earth' is in the third part of the prophecies of Isaiah (65.17f.). The poet provides a vision of a time when people will see the fulfilment of God's original vision for the creation: a human community life with God, suffused with joy; in which long life replaces premature death; in which there is fulfilment in work and creativity instead of toil. God will live in fellowship with his people, and the whole created order will be healed: 'The wolf and the lamb shall feed together, the lion shall eat straw like the ox; but the serpent – its food shall be dust! They shall not hurt or destroy on all my holy mountain, says the LORD' (65.25f.). The vision is of personal, social and ecological harmony in community with God, a vision of *shalom*.

That vision is not yet fulfilled. It is picked up by the last book in the Bible, the Revelation to John, where battles are still to be fought, both on earth and in heaven, to secure God's victory over evil and decay. But the vision remains of the new heaven and the new earth, where God is at home with mortals. 'He will dwell with them; they will be his people, and God himself will be with them; he will wipe every tear from their eyes. Death will be no more; mourning and crying and pain will be no more, for the first things have passed away' (Rev. 21.1f.). It is a vision of what will one day be, lit by the glory of God's throne – and leads to the longing prayer, 'Amen. Come, Lord Jesus!' (Rev. 22.20).

It is this eschatological perspective which holds together God's purposes for the whole of his creation, and his purposes of love for his people. It is this perspective which should drive the church forwards in hope in its worship, work and witness. N.T. Wright writes this:

> Christian hope, therefore, is for a full, recreated life in the presence and love of God, a totally renewed creation, an integrated new heavens and new earth, and a complete humanness – complete not in and for itself as an isolated entity, but complete in worship and love for God, complete in love for one another as humans, complete in stewardship over God's world, and so, and only in that complete context, a full humanness in itself.[12]

This forward perspective on the creation reshapes our understanding of humanity's role within the world in several ways. In the first place, this perspective underlines powerfully that 'the earth is the LORD's and everything that is in it'. This is not our world, at our disposal. Our place is a more humble one of ethical obedience and covenant allegiance. Secondly, it is God who will bring about a new order of creation; we cannot save the world – we are called to obedient faithfulness and to bear

---

12 N.T. Wright, *New Heavens, New Earth*, 1999, p. 24.

witness. Thirdly, we are not autonomous beings with the burden of finding our own technological fixes to everything that goes wrong. We are bound to use our science and technology responsibly, and express our allegiance to God by 'serving and protecting' God's creation, and working for justice and neighbour love, but the future of the planet is in God's hands. Fourthly, we can live with hope. There is much to cause a sense of despair and helplessness about the agendas of climate change. The vision of the coming new heaven and new earth holds out before us a hope that God is healing and restoring the creation, and inviting us to be covenant partners in the enterprise. Fifthly, and importantly, the vision of God's future is an added incentive to live and act as responsible covenant partners with God for the future of the earth. There is no hint whatever in the New Testament that because God is the sovereign Lord, we should merely relax and leave everything to God. The emphasis is all the other way: 'Work out your salvation, because God is at work' (Phil. 2.12–13). The perspective of the end time rather motivates us to live and work now as signposts to that future,[13] and to live out in the present the values of God's coming kingdom; to live as bearers of hope for the world.

We are to live, in other words, as we pray, that God's kingdom will come on earth as it is in heaven. We do not know how the created order will be transformed, or how heaven and earth will come together. We do know that in our mission of sharing in God's redemptive purpose for the world, those actions of ours which mirror God's generous giving, faithful love, commitment to justice, healing and redeeming grace will play their part in the new creation.

The 'end' of the world and the hope of resurrection

It is not easy to relate the visions of the prophets to the predictions of cosmologists about the future of the planet, whose

---

13 F. Bridger, 'Ecology and Eschatology', in *Tyndale Bulletin* 41.2 (1990), p. 301.

long-term history seems to be determined by the competing effects of expansion from the big bang, and gravitational forces drawing everything together into what may, eventually, be a 'big crunch'. It is not easy to bring the timescales of human history into resonance with the thousands of millions of years of cosmic reality. As scientist-theologian John Polkinghorne argues in *The God of Hope and the End of the World*,[14] although the universe appears to have been lifeless for 11 billion years, 'there is a real sense in which it was pregnant with the possibility of life from the very beginning'. Yet God's gift of life formed a new beginning. There is no reason to deny that God's creative power can again do new things within an evolving universe. In fact, in Polkinghorne's own exploration of what a new heaven and a new earth might mean in physical scientific terms, he speaks both of transience (that everything will change) and preservation (that God will keep and transform everything that is good about this present world so that it will become the new creation).

One image of what this might mean is perhaps given to us in the narrative of the transfiguration of Christ on the mountain, when three of the disciples saw Jesus' appearance changed and his clothes dazzling white (Luke 9.28f.). The Eastern Church sees much more significance in this event than the Western Church has tended to see, and believes the Transfiguration is first an affirmation 'of the worth of the sensible and of matter', as Christ's divine glory was seen in his earthly body. But then the Transfiguration of Christ is also seen as a symbol of the resurrection bodies of Christians, and beyond that, a symbol of the 'Transfiguration of the world' and the restoration to creation of its true order.[15]

It is St Paul's teaching about resurrection, though, with its stress on continuity and transformation, particularly the resur-

---

14 John Polkinghorne, *The God of Hope and the End of the World*, 2002.

15 Anestis Keselopoulos, *Man and the Environment: A Study of St Symeon the New Theologian*, 2001, pp. 4f.

rection of Jesus Christ, which gives us the main clues we have about what resurrection may mean for the rest of the created order. In his classic discussion in 1 Corinthians 15, Paul uses the example of a seed in the ground: 'God gives it a body as he has chosen, and to each kind of seed its own body'. And he develops the thought that the seed dies in the ground, and in its place comes up a glorious flower. There is continuity – the life from the seed is continuous with the life of that particular flower. But there is transformation – from the darkness of the earth to the bright colours of the fresh air. So it is, he says, with the resurrection of the dead. In ways we do not know and cannot predict, the Creator God will resurrect this world order into a new heaven and a new earth, in recognizable continuity with this present world but transformed into a new order of being. That, says St Paul, is the basis for the Christian hope.

It is this hope which then drives St Paul to urge his readers to work even harder in the cause of the Gospel: 'Therefore, my beloved, be steadfast, immovable, always excelling in the work of the Lord, because you know that in the Lord your labour is not in vain' (1 Cor. 15.58).

The task of the Christian community, created by the death and resurrection of Jesus, drawn together in the Eucharist, is to hold that hope for the world, and on the basis of that hope bear witness to God and live and act in the light of his coming kingdom.

7

Gift and calling: living as God's covenant people

> May we who share Christ's body live his risen life;
> we who drink his cup bring life to others;
> we whom the Spirit lights give light to the world.
> Keep us firm in the hope you have set before us,
> so we and all your children will be free,
> and the whole earth live to praise your name;
> through Jesus Christ our Lord.
>
> Common Worship, Holy Communion

The 'covenant' theme holds together a Christian response to many of the questions posed for us by climate change. It gives us a perspective on our human relationships to the rest of God's creation. It offers us a Sabbath vision of 'the sacred', of joy and sufficiency. It calls us back to living sustainably and justly, and gives us a basis for hope in God's future.

The covenant comes to its climax in the Upper Room in Jerusalem where Jesus institutes the Lord's Supper, and supremely in his death and resurrection. The calling to be God's covenant people is now to be lived out in his Church, the Body of Christ, energized by the Spirit, nourished through the Word and Sacrament. The Eucharist also holds many of these themes together. It unites creation and the covenant of redemption – the natural world and the world of people. The ordinary bread 'which earth has given', and ordinary wine, 'the fruit of the vine' – gifts of God's creation – become for us the bread of life and the cup of salvation. The Eucharist holds out before us the vision of a sacred holy feast of sufficiency, in which angels, archangels and all the company of heaven share, reminding us of the holiness of God and the sanctity of God's world, and inviting us to delight in God's joy. It reminds us of God's law and our sin, our need for penitence and God's forgiveness, the centrality of love, and the prayer of hope that the day will come 'when justice and mercy shall be seen in all the world'. It is centred on the self-giving love of God for the world and for us, the body and blood of Christ given for our healing, and the healing of creation. Behind the Christian eucharistic liturgy lie the rituals of the Day of Atonement, in which through the gift of sacrifice, sin is forgiven, creation is restored and the covenant renewed (Lev. 16; Heb. 9–10).[1] In the Eucharist more clearly than anywhere else, heaven and earth come together in a foretaste of God's coming kingdom and the resurrection of all things into his love and his life. The liturgy ends with a commitment to a renewed allegiance, and the prayer that God would send us out into the world in the power of the Spirit to live and work to God's praise and glory.

One of the interesting features of St Paul's teaching about the Lord's Supper in the church in Corinth is that it comes in the context of division. There were splits within the Christian community, and it seems from Paul's description of what was going on that this resulted in divisions, even during the sharing of Holy Communion. Whereas in some homes there would be a division between the richer guests who dined with the host in the main room, and poorer visitors who were left in the atrium outside – all symbolic of the 'honour-shame' culture of the Roman Empire – it seems that this division between rich and poor, the haves and the have-nots, was being carried over into times when the dinner at home merged into the Lord's Supper. By this, says Paul, 'you show contempt for the church of God and humiliate those who have nothing' (1 Cor. 11.22). He goes on to argue that all who eat the bread and drink the cup of the Lord in the Eucharist, which he describes as 'the new covenant in my blood', must 'discern the body' (1 Cor. 11.29), which

---

1 Cf. Margaret Barker, *The Great High Priest*, 2003.

almost certainly means 'recognize what characterizes the body [i.e. the Body of Christ] as different'.[2] In other words, he is saying 'be very mindful of the way of Jesus Christ – he gave himself for others in sheer grace'. The Lord's Supper underlines our sharing and identifying with the crucified Jesus Christ – and that must promote social transformation; that means there should be no more 'haves and have-nots'; all are to be treated equally and justly in the light of Christ's generous gift. That is a sobering word for our world in which poverty, disease, hunger and therefore disadvantage and resentment are growing.

Our primary task, therefore, as the people of God is to follow the way of Jesus Christ. This means to demonstrate in our life and worship, work and witness, that it is possible to 'live the new life, following the commandments of God and walking in his holy ways', a life which displays the relationship between the Creator and God's creation, and is lived out in justice and love to our neighbours, especially those who are poor and disadvantaged. This is a life which receives God's creation as covenanted gift and seeks responsibly to fulfil our calling to serve it and protect it, which lives by the Sabbath principle of sufficiency and joyful generosity, and a life-giving rhythm of work and worship, which seeks to do justice, love mercy and walk humbly with God, and in the light of the redeeming grace of Christ lives in hope of resurrection.

Mission

This is the Church's mission in relation to creation, and in response to the questions posed for us by climate change. We remind ourselves again of the psalmist's word, 'The earth is the Lord's and all that is in it' (Ps. 24.1), and of how Jesus takes this sense of ownership and sovereignty to himself: 'All authority in heaven and on earth has been given to me' (Matt. 28.18). This is not our world at our disposal; it is God's world, given to us as

---

2 A.C. Thiselton, *The First Epistle to the Corinthians*, 2000, p. 893.

GIFT AND CALLING

a gift of God's covenanted love, and we have been given a responsible calling of royal service and priestliness to serve it and protect it. Archbishop Rowan Williams put it like this:

> It is common to describe the vocation of human beings in this context as 'liturgical': human beings orchestrate the reflection of God's glory in the world by clothing material things with sacred meaning and presenting the world before God in prayer. Worship is not only a matter of words, but is a foretaste of the God-related destiny of the world, that longed-for state of creation in which everything can be clearly seen as bearing God's glory and love . . .
>
> What most deeply and basically is is the self-giving action of God; everything that happens to exist, everything that belongs in the interlocking pattern of the intelligible world, is, and is the way it is, in virtue of the underlying reality which is God's giving . . . The secret at the heart of all things is gift; and the purpose of God in so giving a share in his action, an 'analogical' echo of his own life, is that what is not God may be suffused with God's joy.[3]

In response to God's gift, our human calling has been appropriately understood by Christopher Wright in his magisterial *The Mission of God* as part of the Church's mission in the contemporary world. He argues strongly that what he calls 'creation care', and especially justice towards the earth and compassion in relation to human need, are centrally part of the mission of the Gospel. He discusses 'ecological concern and environmental action as legitimate integral dimensions of biblical mission', and he suggests with regard to such forms of action that:

- they are responding to an urgent global issue
- they are expressions of our love and obedience to God the Creator

---

3 Rowan Williams, *Environment Lecture 'Changing the Myths we Live By'*, 5 July 2004, www.archbishopofcanterbury.org/1168

- they restore our proper priestly and kingly role in relation to the earth
- they expose and expand our motivation for holistic mission
- they constitute a contemporary prophetic opportunity for the Church
- they embody the core biblical values of compassion and justice.[4]

Of the Five Marks of Mission adopted by the Anglican Consultative Council, and widely used, the fifth mark is this:

- to strive to safeguard the integrity of creation and sustain and renew the life of the earth.

What, then, in practical terms might the Church's actions in mission include, living out our calling in response to God's creation gift?

Practical action

Our primary task, as we have already said, is to live as the people of God, following the way of Jesus Christ, and through our worship, work and witness embody a style of life which reflects the truth about God, about creation as his gift, about our role as royal servants and priests. That style of life should include putting our own house in order as a church nationally and locally, and learning as church communities to live sustainably and fairly.

This will involve very radical change. It will not be easy; it will be costly; it will involve sacrifice. Living out our calling may include political lobbying of government at all levels. It could mean involvement in local community decisions and priorities, it could include practical action in dioceses and parishes, as well as at the family and individual level. It must include a serious

---

4 C.J.H. Wright, *The Mission of God*, p. 419.

evaluation of the social values and economic priorities by which we live. But the Christian's first task is to recover a sense of our calling to a radical discipleship of allegiance to the Lord Jesus Christ – to be and to live in hope as the covenant people of God.

Discipleship

In his book *Dissident Discipleship*,[5] David Augsburger argues that a fully biblical understanding of discipleship essentially includes the dimensions of commitment to love and service of our neighbours and of the world around us. There is no separation between obedience to God and solidarity with the world. The Christian commitment to prayer goes hand in hand with the Christian commitment to service. The first letter of John puts it very starkly: 'The commandment we have from him is this: those who love God must love their brothers and sisters also' (4.21). That includes brothers and sisters in sub-Saharan Africa now, and brothers and sisters yet to be born. This is part of our response to the God who 'so loved the world'.

This is the heavy responsibility placed on us all every time we celebrate the Eucharist. Our worshipping life together, which unites us afresh with the self-giving love of God in Christ, should be moulding us together into the Body of Christ in a lifestyle which shares that love generously in and for the world – a new humanity living in light and hope and freedom, in justice and in compassion, so that, as the prayer puts it, 'the whole earth may live to praise God's name'.

As the Body of Christ we bear witness to our faith and to the truth about the world and about humanity as we understand it. In relation to climate change, that witness needs to be at different levels. I cannot discuss here the huge range of suggestions that have been made about what actions governments, societies or individuals can or should take. I can simply dip into the huge

---

5 David Augsburger, *Dissident Discipleship*, 2006.

bran tub and pick out a small selection of some of what seem to me the most obvious or effective things we as Christian people can do. We can bear witness at government level about global justice in adaptation to climate change, and in relation to national legislation; we can bear witness at our local community level concerning priorities in the use of local resources; we can bear witness through our corporate life together as congregations of worshipping people, and through decisions we make in our schools, families and personal lives. Much more could be said, which would need more space or competence than I have. I hope this much will inform our prayers and hopefully our actions in our living out our allegiance as disciples of Jesus Christ in our contemporary context, and in the growing urgency of the question posed for us by climate change.

Bearing witness to government on global issues

We recall that the 1998 Lambeth Conference of Anglican bishops called on ecumenical partners, other faith communities, governments and transnational companies:

- to work for a sustainable society in a sustainable world
- to recognize the dignity and rights of all people and the sanctity of all life, especially the rights of future generations
- to ensure the responsible use and recyling of natural resources
- to bring about economic reforms which will establish a just and fair trading system both for people and for the environment.

These are still pertinent goals, brought into even sharper focus now than they were in 1998.

To work for a sustainable society in a sustainable world in response to climate change has to bring the environmental agenda and the development agenda together. We have argued the need to work for justice in the tasks of achieving sustainable development, mitigation and adaptation. The crucial issue was well put in *Fairness in Adaptation to Climate Change* by Neil

Adger and his co-authors: 'a society is just only if it enables improvement in the position of the least advantaged'.[6]

Part of our Christian witness – whether as Christian people who work in government or transnational corporations, or as Christian voters, shareholders or writers of letters to Members of Parliament – is to hold the requirements of justice before our legislators and those who influence the economies of the world. Christian people may be in a position to argue for justice from our government on the global scene – perhaps to argue for 'Contraction and Convergence', or other models seeking fairness in mitigation and in adaptation. Whichever priorities are chosen, the same overall obligation remains: 'seeking fair outcomes for the survival of the natural world'.

Bearing witness on national issues

In addition to government responsibilities in relation to the global economy, it needs also to legislate for national priorities, both for the care and protection of the environment, and in relation to energy needs and resources. Urgent decisions are going to be needed in the UK about the latter, and about binding efficiency standards, and many will need legislation to enforce them.

The Tyndall Centre for Climate Change Research published the result of research[7] which was set up to see if it is possible to live within a carbon budget dictated by climate change while at the same time allowing the economy to grow. They developed a series of scenarios with different variables in energy demands and in energy sources (renewables, fossil fuels with carbon capture and storage, biomass, nuclear), and various priorities for energy use (passenger and goods transport, and household consumption). Their conclusion was that the government's

---

6 Adger et al. (eds), *Fairness in Adaptation to Climate Change*, p. ix.
7 for Friends of the Earth and the Cooperative Bank, published as *Living Within a Carbon Budget*, July 2006, Tyndall Centre (www.tyndall.ac.uk/publications).

(then) target of 60% reduction in carbon dioxide emission by 2050 would be achievable – even that the higher target of 90% by 2050 and 70% by 2030 is achievable, but would need significant government action. There would need to be a break in the link between energy consumption and carbon dioxide emissions. We would need to reduce energy demand as well as work for energy efficiency. It was assumed that all sectors (household, industry, services and transport) would be brought under some sort of emissions trading scheme or carbon tax at the earliest opportunity. There would need to be an integrated transport policy in line with an energy policy. The exclusion so far of emissions from international air travel has led to misleading conclusions about emissions targets. Aviation and shipping energy consumption would need to be included, as aviation is the fastest growing sector and will be the most significant by 2050 on current trends. Some parts of government are advocating significant carbon reductions while others are supporting considerable growth in air travel. What is needed is a coherent climate policy.[8]

It is clear from this research that urgent government action is needed. This is not mainly about achieving a certain reduction in percentage by the year 2050; it is about significantly reducing the total quantity of carbon dioxide emitted between now and 2050. Their conclusion for policy-makers is stark:

> In waiting for technology or the EU ETS to offer a smooth transition to a low-carbon future, we are deluding ourselves. It is an act either of negligence or irresponsibility for policy-makers continually to refer to a 2050 target as the key driver in addressing climate change. The real challenge we face is in making the radical shift onto a low-carbon pathway by 2010–12, and thereafter driving down carbon intensity at an unprecedented 9% per annum, for up to two decades. The urgency with which we must make the transition to a low-

---

8 Cf. K. Anderson, S. Shackley, S. Mander and A. Bows, *Decarbonising the UK*, 2005.

carbon pathway leaves no option but to instigate a radical and immediate programme of demand management. It is incumbent on government to initiate, maintain and monitor this programme whilst simultaneously facilitating a phased transition to low-carbon demand and supply technologies.[9]

Are we to rely on imported gas from Nigeria, Russia, North Africa or the Gulf States which will raise carbon dioxide emissions, or to invest in nuclear power (with the fears it raises concerning the disposal of waste), or indeed to invest heavily in renewable energy sources such as wind-turbines, or revert to coal in the hope of developing adequate technologies for capturing the carbon emitted? It is salutary that about one-third of our energy consumption in the UK is from domestic use, about one-third from transport, and one-third from industry.

One of the most articulate, if controversial, protagonists for urgent government action in the UK is George Monbiot. His passionate book *Heat* argues that it would be just about possible in the UK to reduce our carbon emissions by 90% by 2030, and outlines a series of steps which, he argues, need to be taken. I will give a brief summary of these, not because I can judge whether they are all right or workable, but because they illustrate the sorts of national issues to which Christian people need to give their attention in their prayers and in bearing witness to justice and compassion.[10]

- Set an annual personal carbon ration for each citizen – a free annual quota of carbon dioxide which can be spent on gas or electricity, petrol, train or plane tickets. If they run out, they must buy more from someone who has some to spare.
- Introduce a new set of building regulations to impose strict energy-efficient requirements on all major refurbishments; to bring all rented property up to high, energy-efficient stan-

---

9 *Living Within a Carbon Budget*, p. 162.
10 George Monbiot, *Heat*, 2006, and summarised in George Monbiot, 'Save the planet in ten steps', *The Guardian*, 30 October 2006.

dards before they can be let out; to ensure all new homes are built to a standard which requires no heating system other than sunlight – the Germans have developed a *passivhaus* prototype.
- Ban the sale of incandescent lightbulbs, patio heaters, garden floodlights, and introduce heavy taxes on the least efficient electronic goods.
- Redeploy the money earmarked for new nuclear missiles towards massive investment in energy generation and distribution – such as off-shore wind farms and a hydrogen pipeline network.
- Promote a new national coach network based on motorway junctions, with coaches on dedicated motorway lanes, and urban public transport networks extended to meet them.[11]
- Oblige all chains of filling stations to supply leasable electric car batteries.
- Stop road building and road widening.
- Reduce UK airport capacity and work for a significant reduction in flying. In *Heat*, Monbiot argues that we need to stop flying altogether: 'It has become plain to me that long-distance travel, high speed and the curtailment of climate change are not compatible. If you fly, you destroy other people's lives.'[12] His one concession is travel to see overseas loved-ones.
- Legislate for the closure of out-of-town superstores and their replacement with a warehouse and delivery system.

Other people have produced other lists of actions which could cumulatively produce a large effect on carbon emissions. For example, improving the fuel efficiency of cars; halving the miles travelled by car each year; transferring much of our freight from road to rail; increasing the efficiency of heating,

---

[11] This is based on an idea developed by Alan Storkey. See www.publications.parliament.uk/pa/cm200506/cmselect/cmtran/1317/1317am04.htm

[12] Monbiot, *Heat*, p. 188.

lighting, cooling and appliances; improving the efficiency of coal-fired power stations; introducing a system of carbon-capture from power stations and storing it underground; replacing many coal-fired power stations with natural gas-fired plants; seriously considering whether the risks of nuclear power are outweighed by the benefits of using nuclear energy instead of fossil fuels at least in the mid-term; increasing wind-generated power; increasing the use of solar power; making hydrogen fuel for cars; considering whether the use of biofuels would be beneficial, given the adverse affect they may have on food production; stopping all deforestation; legislating to reduce food miles; introducing a carbon tax for everyone. Any such actions will require government legislation to make them happen – but they are not vote-winners.

The national task also includes, for example, preparing for coastal erosion, getting used to different patterns of agriculture, planning how to handle the migration of people who will have been flooded out of their homes and livelihoods through the likely rise in ocean levels. How can the national and local church contribute effectively to such discussions?

Bearing witness as a local church

Partnership with other churches

One of the good things about the Anglican Communion is the scheme called Partnership for World Mission, and in particular its arrangement of 'companion links'. Rather like the twinning of towns, these links associate dioceses and parishes with others in other parts of the world. So Norwich Diocese has a companion link with Papua New Guinea; Southwark Diocese is linked with three of the dioceses of Zimbabwe.

Their purpose is to support, challenge and assist one another across ethnic, regional and national boundaries. To talk and meet with Christians from countries and cultures very different from our own can be very helpful in breaking down insularity, helping us to see things from a different perspective, and noticing the work of the Holy Spirit in different ways in different parts of the world. They enable us to reassess our own priorities, and open to us ways of receiving insight and help from the world Church. The formation of local covenants of commitment from one diocese or one parish to another strengthens bonds of affection, friendship and prayer, and can inform our different perspectives on the responses needed to climate change.

Trade justice

Christian Aid and others agencies have contributed to a greater global awareness through their persistent and laudable campaign for trade justice. 'To develop, poor people need trade justice. They need the mountain of hypocritical subsidies in rich countries to be moved; they need the physical barriers of poverty that prevent them from taking advantage of new markets to be swept away; and they need to be supported and protected in the meantime.'[13]

At the local level, to support Fairtrade goods and to put pressure on our shops and supermarkets to sell more, could be an expression of Christian discipleship.

An imaginative project in relation to bottled water is the establishment of Belu.[14] Over the past century, two-thirds of available fresh water on the planet had been used or polluted. Now, a quarter of the people on earth do not have access to clean water. Belu was launched to try to address this. In cooperation with Water Aid, Belu bottles water from springs in Shropshire and in the Black Mountains in corn-based bio-bottles (which can be commercially composted) for sale in the UK. All its profts are donated to fund clean water projects in the UK and around the world, the first of which was in Tamil Nadu. They say that every bottle of Belu purchased in the UK provides clean water for one person in Tamil Nadu for one month. This

---

13 Christian Aid, *Taking Liberties*, 2004.
14 www.belu.org

cuts down on imported bottled water from the continent – with its carbon transport costs, and from their profits provides a carbon-neutral access to clean water for many people.

Food miles

Near where I live, the local farm shop sells local butter, local milk, eggs and vegetables, and a local supermarket has recently announced that it will use only local produce in its breadmaking. By contrast, apples from Australia and New Zealand are flown to America to be sold in supermarkets in Los Angeles, while apples from California are flown across the Atlantic to be sold in supermarkets in the UK. This has to be nonsense. Each tonne of food or goods or livestock is now travelling within the UK 20% more than it did in 1990. It is hard to believe the amount of miles covered by some vegetables from the fields in which they are grown to the place where they are stored and sorted in a different part of the country, then to the place where they are packed in another different part of the country, and then to the distribution depot in yet another different place before reaching the shops. In his brave 2005 guide to ethical living *A Good Life*,[15] Leo Hickman produced some worrying statistics.

- 45% of our food in the UK is imported from abroad
- a kiwi flown from New Zealand to Britain leads to five times its own weight in greenhouse gas emissions
- the more food is transported the more it needs to be packaged; and one-sixth of what we pay in the UK for food goes on packaging: £470 per household per year
- some supermarkets classify 'local' food as that 'grown in the UK'.

He then wrote: 'To illustrate how acute the problem of food miles has become, in 2003 *The Guardian* bought a basket of

---

15 Leo Hickman, *A Good Life*, 2005.

fresh food containing 20 items. It included pears from Argentina, peas from South Africa, tomatoes from Saudi Arabia and lettuce from Spain. The cumulative distance travelled by the contents of the basket was a staggering 100,943 miles – just under half the distance to the moon.'[16] How much energy was used in that shopping trip? It must be part of our Christian discipleship to object to this stupidity.

Red meat

One other dimension to our discipleship could be to consider cutting down on eating red meat. At present there are about two billion domesticated cows on the planet, a huge proportion of which are beef cattle. Their consumption of grain requires huge areas for feed crops, a contributory factor in deforestation. If all the grain fed to animals was available for human use, there would food enough to feed many starving people. The methane emitted from cows' stomachs also contributes significantly to global warming, as methane is a powerful greenhouse gas. All in all the energy used in meat production (cattle feed, slaughter, butchering, transport and sales) is significant. I heard a statistic reported on US television which I have no way of verifying, though I think it is worth repeating for its element of surprise: if every American person, it was said, gave up one meat meal a week, the energy saved that week would be the equivalent to taking 12 million cars off the road.[17]

Waste

One of the issues on which local churches can engage creatively with local councils is on the management of waste. The UK produces around 330 million tonnes of waste annually – a quarter

---

16 Hickman, *A Good Life*, p. 18.
17 Although this needs to be offset by some energy increase in the compensatory food eaten.

of which is from households and business. The rest comes from construction and demolition, sewage sludge, farm waste and spoils from mines and dredging of rivers. In autumn 2007, the Revd John Hale, a vicar in West Sussex, undertook a sabbatical research project drawing on his former expertise in waste management. His report, 'Opportunities for the Church to Promote Sustainable Waste Management in England', concludes that

> The church is well-equipped spiritually, and well-placed geographically (having a 'branch' in every community), to promote the culture-change to waste reduction, re-use of waste, and waste recycling / composting. This can be done by building on churches' existing strengths in doing recycling / composting and working with the community sector and local government, and in making available church land for the new waste facilities that we all need.

Eco-congregations

The Christian responsibility to serve and protect creation is the concern of the organization Eco-Congregation, which has developed sets of resources and worship material designed to help churches identify and affirm their existing environmental ministry and to decide on priorities for the future. One such resource is the 'Church Check-up' (www.ecocongregation.org), a brief audit of the life and ministry of the local church. There is an award scheme to help churches consider environmental issues in the context of their Christian life and mission and take positive action. The audit covers, for example, inviting churches to consider their:

- worship: prayer and music celebrating creation; sorrow for harm done to the environment
- theology: study and preaching programmes
- children's work which can inform, inspire and encourage young people

- youth work, considering debate, conservation projects
- all-age and adult education
- church property: e.g. monitoring energy consumption, care with timetabling meetings, using low-energy lightbulbs, saving water, building maintenance
- church management: check the environmental policy of your bank; ethical investments, use of recycled paper and fairly traded products; local produce in catering; minimizing waste
- church land: the need for wildlife-friendly management; provision for outdoor worship; an area for recreation
- personal lifestyle: encouraging parishioners in their personal lives
- community outreach: establishing links with community organizations and participating in local environmental initiatives
- overseas concerns: living simply that others may simply live; supporting the work of Christian development agencies, promoting fair trade.

Church schools

Many schools, including church schools, are leading the way in environmental concerns. Some dioceses offer award schemes for imaginative environmental projects. There are schools resources available to assist teachers and governors, both in relation to environmental care and energy saving and efficiency. These initiatives are to be encouraged, and the more co-operation that can take place between a church school and the parish in which it is based, the better.

For one local village school, served by a road with no pavement, all the children had to be delivered by car, leading to considerable congestion and safety problems as well as carbon emissions. Then the local farmer kindly donated a small stretch of land alongside the road on which a path and cycle track could be made. Now 100% of (much healthier) children walk or cycle to school.

Diocesan advisory and property committees

All dioceses have a statutory advisory committee concerned with the maintenance of church buildings, and usually a property committee concerned with other property owned or maintained by the diocese. Many are now working to implement diocesan environmental policies, to reduce energy use and increase energy efficiency. Solar panels on south-facing church roofs do not always please architects or heritage bodies, but in many cases they could be much more effective than heating a church building for one or two hours a week with fossil fuels.

Some churches are exploring conservation areas in their use of churchyards, energy efficient boilers, geothermal heating, composting toilets and the use of low-energy lightbulbs. They are seriously considering whether floodlights should be kept only for very special occasions. Some property committees are seeking to make all new-build parsonages low-energy buildings, and where possible to upgrade existing parsonages with insulation, double glazing and energy-efficient heating systems. It is desirable for every such committee to have a written formulated policy about energy efficiency which becomes part of an environmental audit on a regular basis.

Bearing witness at the individual and family level

The primary witness is living a simplified, hopeful, Christian lifestyle which contributes to serving and protecting God's creation, celebrates with joy the sacredness of the world, finds contentment in sufficiency, and strives for justice in all our affairs. Within that, energy saving is a matter of current urgency. Many people feel that the tasks are so large, and the scale so overwhelming, that it seems as though any small gestures they might make will be insignificant.

It is true that the benefits of changing a lightbulb will be insignificant in relation to the carbon costs of flying to Tenerife on holiday, but the surprising fact is that one-third of our energy use in the UK is domestic. If each person were to make some reductions in their energy use, not only might they benefit themselves financially but also their cumulative effects could very significant. If everyone in the UK were to turn off just one stand-by machine at the wall each night, the energy saved would be equivalent to the output of one power station. All our small efforts together can make a huge difference – not just to us and our wallets, but to the health of the planet and the benefit of our neighbours worldwide.

At the University of East Anglia, the Carbon Reduction Project CRed has been working for some years on carbon reduction measures, and has produced useful information about energy saving at home. Of the energy used in the home, about 60% is used on heating. Adding up all the energy used on heating, appliances, cooking, on food and other purchases, and the services we use, CRed calculates that 'an average Norfolk resident is responsible for releasing 9.3 tonnes of carbon dioxide every year – that is roughly five well-filled hot-air balloons'. The capacity of the planet is between 2 and 4 tonnes per person.

Alongside the personal decisions which need to be made about saving in automobile energy costs, and about the use of aircraft (on which CRed has some advice), the energy saving measures which CRed recommends at home include:

- covering pans when cooking
- boiling only the amount of water you need
- choosing locally grown food that is in season
- turning off TVs, videos, DVDs, phone chargers at the wall (an excess of £230 million of the nation's electricity bills are spent on appliances left on standby!)
- avoiding using a dishwasher, or at least using the lowest temperature setting
- hanging washing outside on fine days rather than using a tumble drier[18]

---

18 The financial benefits are not insignificant, either. This action alone could save between £50 and £100 on household bills in a year.

- defrosting your freezer regularly to ensure efficiency
- turning lights off when not in use
- reaching for a jumper before turning up the thermostat
- going for a shower rather than a bath
- changing to a green energy tariff
- fitting low-energy lightbulbs
- draughtproofing windows, doors, loft hatch
- making sure loft is insulated.

On the CRed website (www.cred-uk.org) – indeed, on many other organizations' websites – there is an audit which churches, families, individuals can undertake. It helps us measure our carbon emissions, and helps us judge what changes we can make, small though they may seem, which added together will make a significant difference. Though the task is huge, the task is manageable – and urgent.

Conclusion

God's covenant people, united by the Spirit of Jesus Christ, and sustained by God's Word and the sacrament of the Eucharist are called as disciples to be witnesses – to God's gifts in creation, and to the truth about our human relationship with the natural order. The Eucharist is centred on the loving self-sacrifice of Jesus Christ, and requires of us a sacrificial discipleship. The questions put to us by climate change require answers that will be costly and painful. The tasks are not easy.

What, then, are our tasks as the people of God? First, to recover our vision, and secondly radically to bring our lifestyle into line with our calling as disciples of Jesus Christ. The vision is of a sustainable world community in a sustainable environment. It is rooted in a vision of the natural world as God's creation which humanity has a calling to serve and to protect as God's royal servants and priests. This is a vision of creation as a gift of God's covenanted love which places on us the obligation of a response of justice and neighbour love – to live generously in response to God's generosity. The vision is of the whole created order coming to its fulfilment in Christ, and our calling is to live joyously and hopefully in the light of God's coming kingdom.

But, secondly, this will necessitate changes at every level of our corporate and individual lives. Our task as Christians is not to try ourselves to carry the responsibility for changing the world, for this is God's world. But we are called to play our part in serving it and protecting it. And we are called to bear witness – to the truth about God's world and our human calling, at the level of government and the global economy, and at national and local community levels. Our witness needs to be seen in our local churches and in our personal lifestyles.

But over and above all this we need a widespread repentance and change of heart from the finance-driven consumer/waste culture which is killing the planet. A recovery of the sacred gift of God's creation and the sacredness of our human calling to serve and protect it will deepen our prayer that God would continue to give us – and give to our neighbours across the world and to future generations yet unborn – our daily bread; that God would forgive us our sins and deliver us from evil.

May God's kingdom come on earth as it is in heaven. And may God give each of us the grace, as disciples of Jesus Christ, to respond with generous and unselfish lives to God's gracious gift – and give us the wisdom, courage and joyous motivation to make the small or larger changes we are able to in our lifestyles in the light of his kingdom.

The Church of England Service of Holy Communion closes with the prayer that through Christ we offer to God 'our souls and bodies to be a living sacrifice'. May God send us out in the power of the Spirit to live and work to God's praise and glory.

> O Lord, how manifold are your works! In wisdom you have made them all; the earth is full of your creatures . . .
>
> These all look to you to give them their food in due season . . .

GIFT AND CALLING

When you send forth your spirit they are created; and you renew the face of the earth.

from Psalm 104.24–30

By an Act of the Understanding therefore be present now with all the Creatures among which you live; and hear them in their beings and operations praising God . . .

You are never what you ought till you go out of yourself and walk among them.

from *Centuries of Meditation*, Thomas Traherne

The world is charged with the grandeur of God.
    It will flame out, like shining from shook foil;
    It gathers to a greatness, like the ooze of oil
Crushed. Why do men then now not reck his rod?
Generations have trod, have trod, have trod;
    And all is seared with trade; bleared, smeared with toil;
    And wears man's smudge and shares man's smell: the soil
Is bare now, nor can foot feel, being shod.

And for all this, nature is never spent;
    There lives the dearest freshness deep down things;
And though the last lights off the black West went
    Oh, morning, at the brown brink eastward, springs –
Because the Holy Ghost over the bent
    World broods with warm breast and with ah! bright wings.

God's Grandeur, Gerard Manley Hopkins

Further Reading and Resources

Books

Adger, W. Neil, Jouni Paavola, Saleemul Huq and M.J. Mace (eds), *Fairness in Adaptation to Climate Change*, MIT Press, Cambridge, MA, and London, 2006

Anderson, K., S. Shackley, S. Mander and A. Bows, *Decarbonising the UK: Energy for a Climate Conscious Future*, The Tyndall Centre, University of East Anglia, 2005

Atkinson, David, *The Message of Genesis 1–11*, IVP, Leicester, 1990

— *The Message of Job*, IVP, Leicester, 1991

Augsburger, David, *Dissident Discipleship: a spirituality of self-surrender, love of God and love of neighbor*, Brazos Press, Grand Rapids, MI, 2006

Barker, Margaret, *The Great High Priest*, T&T Clark, Edinburgh, 2003

Barth, K., *Church Dogmatics* (5 vols), T&T Clark, Edinburgh, 1957–77

Barton, John, *Ethics and the Old Testament: the 1997 Diocese of British Columbia John Albert Hall lectures at the Centre for Studies in Religion and Society in the University of Victoria*, SCM, London, 1998

Berry, R.J. (ed.), *The Care of Creation: focusing concern and action*, IVP Leicester, 2000

Berry, R.J., *God's Book of Works: The Nature and Theology of Nature: Glasgow Gifford lectures*, T&T Clark, London, 2003

Bouma-Prediger, Steven, *The Greening of Theology: the ecological models of Rosemary Radford Ruether, Joseph Sittler and Jürgen Moltmann*, Scholars Press, Atlanta, 1995

Bridger, F. 'Ecology and Eschatology: A Neglected Dimension,' *Tyndale Bulletin* 41 (2:1990), pp. 290–302

Brueggemann, Walter, 'From Dust to Kingship (I Kings 16:2; Genesis 3:19),' *Zeitschrift für die alttestamentliche Wissenschaft* 84 (1972) 1–18

FURTHER READING AND RESOURCES

Calvin, J., *Institutes of Christian Religion*, ed. by J. T. McNeill, (21 vols) The Library of Christian Classics, SCM, London, 1960

Carson, Rachel, *Silent Spring*, Houghton Mifflin, Boston, 1962

Cassuto, U., *A Commentary on the Book of Genesis*, Magnes Press, Jerusalem, 1961

Christian Aid, *The Climate of Poverty: Facts, Fears and Hope*, 2006

— *Truly Inconvenient: Tackling Poverty and Climate Change at Once*, 2007

— *The Human Face of Climate Change*, 2007

Church of England Mission and Public Affairs Council, *Sharing God's Planet*, Church House Publishing, London, 2005

Clifford, Paula, '*All Creation Groaning*': *A Theological Approach to Climate Change and Development*, Christian Aid, 2007

Conradie, Ernst M., *Hope for the Earth: Vistas on a New Century*, Wipf & Stock, Eugene, Oregon, 2000

Dawkins, R., *Unweaving the Rainbow: science, delusion and the appetite for wonder*, Allen Lane, London, 1998

DeWitt, Calvin B., *Earth-Wise: a biblical response to environmental issues*, CRC Publications, Grand Rapids, 1994

Flannery, Tim, *The Weather Makers*, Allen Lane, London, 2005

Foster, C. and D. Shreeve, *How Many Lightbulbs Does it Take to Change a Christian?*, Church House Publishing, London, 2007

Goldingay, John, *New International Biblical Commentary: Isaiah*, Paternoster Press, London, 2001

Gore, Al, *An Inconvenient Truth*, Bloomsbury, London, 2006

Gosling, David, *Religion and Ecology in India and South East Asia*, Routledge, London, 2001

Granberg-Michaelson, W., *Tending the Garden*, Eerdmans, Grand Rapids, 1990

Grey, Mary C., *Sacred Longings: ecofeminist theology and globalisation*, SCM Press, London, 2003

Guillebaud, J., 'Population Growth, Global Warming and Sustainability of the Environment' in *The Bible in Transmission*, Summer 2006, The Bible Society, Swindon

Habgood, John, *The Concept of Nature*, Darton, Longman & Todd, London, 2002

Hendry, George S., *Theology of Nature*, Westminster Press, Philadelphia, 1980

Hessel, D.T. and Rosemary Radford Ruether, *Christianity and Ecology*, Harvard University, 2000

Hickman, Leo, *A Good Life*, Eden Books, London, 2005
Hopkins, Gerard Manley, *Poems and Prose of Gerard Manley Hopkins/ Selected with an introduction and notes by W. H. Gardner*, Penguin, Harmondsworth, 1953
Houghton, John, *Global Warming: The Complete Briefing*, 3rd edn, Cambridge University Press, Cambridge, 2004
Hubbard, David Allan, *The Communicator's Commentary. Proverbs*, Word Books, Dallas, TX, 1989

Intergovernmental Panel on Climate Change, Working Group 1 Contribution to the Fourth Assessment Report, *Climate Change 2007: The Physical Science Basis*, IPCC, 2007

Jones, James, *Jesus and the Earth*, SPCK, London, 2003

Keselopoulos, Anestis, *Man and the Environment: A Study of St Symeon the New Theologian*, St. Vladimir's Seminary Press, Yonkers, NY, 2001
Kidner, Derek, *Psalms 73–150 A Commentary on Books II–IV of the Psalms*, IVP, Leicester, 1975
— *The message of Jeremiah: against wind and tide*, IVP, Leicester, 1987
Küng, H., *On Being a Christian*, translated by Edward Quinn, Collins, London, 1977

Logan, Patrick, *Biblical Reflections on the Political Economy of Jubilee*, Southwark Diocese, 1997
Lovelock, James, *The Revenge of Gaia*, Allen Lane, London, 2006

McGrath, Alister, *A Scientific Theology. I. Nature*, T&T Clark, London, 2001
— *The Re-enchantment of Nature: Science, Religion and the Human Sense of Wonder*, Hodder & Stoughton, London, 2002
McIntosh, Alastair, *Soil and Soul*, Aurum Press, London, 2001
Minns, Denis, *Irenaeus*, Georgetown University Press, Washington DC, 1994
Moltmann, J., *God in Creation: An Ecological Doctrine of Creation*, SCM Press, London, 1985
— *The Trinity and the Kingdom of God: the doctrine of God*, SCM, London, 1981
— *Science and Wisdom*, SCM Press, London, 2003
— *The Future of Creation*, SCM Press, London, 1979
— *The Power of the Powerless*, SCM Press, London, 1981
Monbiot, George, *Heat*, Allen Lane, London, 2006
Murray, Robert, *The Cosmic Covenant*, Sheed & Ward, London, 1992

FURTHER READING AND RESOURCES

Nash, James A., *Loving Nature: ecological integrity and Christian responsibility*, Abingdon Press, Nashville, 1991

Newell, Philip, *Listening for the Heartbeat of God: A Celtic Spirituality*, SPCK, London, 1997

Northcott, Michael S., *A Moral Climate: the ethics of global warming*, Darton, Longman & Todd, London, 2007

Oppenheimer, Helen, *The Character of Christian Morality*, Faith Press, Leighton Buzzard, 1974

Polkinghorne, John, *The God of Hope and the End of the World*, SPCK, London, 2002
— *Science and Providence*, SPCK, London, 1989

Porritt, Jonathon, *Capitalism as if the World Matters*, Earthscan, London, 2005

Rad, Gerhard von, *Genesis, a commentary*, SCM, London, 1963
— *Deuteronomy, a commentary*, SCM, London, 1966

Santmire H. Paul, *Nature Reborn*, Fortress Press, Minneapolis, 2000
— *The Travail of Nature*, Fortress Press, Minneapolis, 1985

Schaeffer, Francis A., *Pollution and the Death of Man: the Christian View of Ecology*, Hodder & Stoughton, London, 1970

Sherrard, Philip, *The Rape of Man and Nature*, Golgonooza Press, Ipswich, 1987

Spencer, N. and R. White, *Christianity, Climate Change and Sustainable Living*, SPCK, London, 2007

Stern, Nicholas, *The Stern Review Report to H M Treasury*, 2006

Taylor, John V., *Enough is Enough*, SCM Press, London, 1975

Temple, William, *Readings in St John's Gospel*, MacMillan, s.l., 1939

The Royal Commission on Environmental Pollution, 22nd Report, *Energy: The Changing Climate*, Crown Copyright 2000

Thiselton, A. C., *The First Epistle to the Corinthians*, Eerdmans, Grand Rapids, MI, 2000

Thomas, Keith, *Man and the Natural World*, Penguin, London, 1984

Thorson, W., 'The Spiritual Dimensions of Science' in *Horizons of Science: Christian scholars speak out* ed. by Carl F. H. Henry, Harper and Row, San Francisco; London, 1978

Traherne, Thomas, *Centuries of Meditations*, A. R. Mowbray, London, 1985

Weiser, A., *The Psalms*, SCM, London, 1962

World Council of Churches, *Solidarity with Victims of Climate Change*, 2002

Wright, C. J. H., *The Mission of God*, IVP, Leicester, 2006
— *Living as the People of God*, IVP, Leicester, 1983
Wright, N.T., *New Heavens, New Earth*, Grove Books, Cambridge, 1999
— *Jesus and the Victory of God*, SPCK, London, 1996
— *Evangelical Anglican Identity: the connection between Bible, Gospel & Church*, Latimer House, Oxford, 1980
— *Paul: In Fresh Perspective*, SPCK, London, 2005

Yoder, John Howard, *The Politics of Jesus*, Eerdmans, Grand Rapids, MI, 1972

Online resources and contacts

www.arocha.org
www.christian-ecology.org.uk
www.conservationfoundation.co.uk
www.ecocongregation.org
www.christiansandclimate.org
www.tyndall.ac.uk
www.cred.org.uk